THE CHILD'S WORLD®

ENCYCLOPEDIA
of BASEBALL

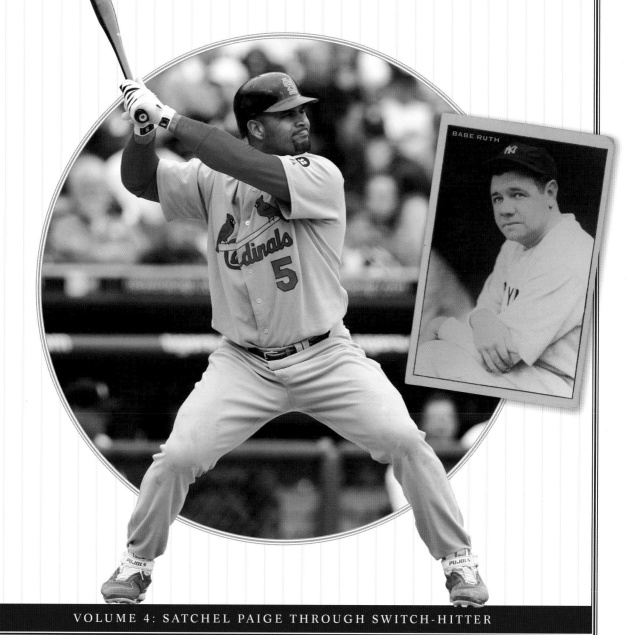

VOLUME 4: SATCHEL PAIGE THROUGH SWITCH-HITTER

By James Buckley, Jr., David Fischer, Jim Gigliotti, and Ted Keith

KEY TO SYMBOLS

Throughout *The Child's World® Encyclopedia of Baseball*, you'll see these symbols. They'll give you a quick clue pointing to each entry's general subject area.

Active player

Baseball word or phrase

Hall of Fame

Miscellaneous

Ballpark

Team

The Child's World
www.childsworld.com

Published in the United States of America by The Child's World®
1980 Lookout Drive, Mankato, MN 56003-1705
800-599-READ • www.childsworld.com

ACKNOWLEDGMENTS

The Child's World®: Mary Berendes, Publishing Director

Produced by Shoreline Publishing Group LLC
President / Editorial Director: James Buckley, Jr.
Cover Design: Kathleen Petelinsek, The Design Lab
Interior Design: Tom Carling, carlingdesign.com
Assistant Editors: Jim Gigliotti, Zach Spear

Cover Photo Credits: Focus on Baseball (main); National Baseball Library (inset).
Interior Photo Credits: AP/Wide World: 6, 7, 16, 18, 19, 21, 22, 23, 25, 26, 35, 40, 46, 47, 51, 52; Corbis: 44, 48, 49, 56, 58, 66, 67, 72, 73, 75, 76, 77, 80, 81; Focus on Baseball: 8, 9, 10, 12, 15, 17, 20, 24, 27, 28, 31, 34, 36, 39, 41, 45, 53, 55, 57, 59, 60, 61, 62, 64, 68, 79, 82, 83; Getty Images: 11, 63; iStock: 29; Library of Congress: 42; Al Messerschmidt: 30; National Baseball Hall of Fame Library: 4, 14, 32, 33, 38, 54, 65, 69, 60, 71, 78; Shoreline Publishing Group: 13, 50

LIBRARY OF CONGRESS CATALOG-IN-PUBLICATION DATA

The Child's World encyclopedia of baseball / by James Buckley, Jr. ... [et al.].
  p. cm. – (The Child's World encyclopedia of baseball)
 Includes index.
 ISBN 978-1-60253-167-3 (library bound : alk. paper)–ISBN 978-1-60253-168-0 (library bound : alk. paper)–ISBN 978-1-60253-169-7 (library bound : alk. paper)–ISBN 978-1-60253-170-3 (library bound : alk. paper)–ISBN 978-1-60253-171-0 (library bound : alk. paper)
 1. Baseball–United States–Encyclopedias, Juvenile. I. Buckley, James, 1963- II. Child's World (Firm) III. Title. IV. Series.

GV867.5.C46 2009
796.3570973–dc22

2008039461

■ *All-time great Honus Wagner.*

P EOPLE HAVE BEEN PLAYING BASEBALL, America's national, pastime, for more than 150 years, so we needed a lot of room to do it justice! The five big volumes of *The Child's World˙ Encyclopedia of Baseball* hold as much as we could squeeze in about this favorite sport.

The Babe. The Say-Hey Kid. The Iron Horse. The Splendid Splinter. Rapid Robert. Hammerin' Hank. You'll read all about these great players of yesterday. You'll also learn about your favorite stars of today: Pujols, Jeter, Griffey, Soriano, Santana, Manny, and Big Papi. How about revisiting some of baseball's most memorable plays and games?

■ *Cardinals hero Albert Pujols.*

The Shot Heard 'Round the World. The Catch. The Grand-Slam Single. You'll find all of these—and more.

Have a favorite big-league team? They're all here, with a complete history for each team that includes its all-time record.

Ever wonder what it means to catch a can of corn, hit a dinger, or use a fungo? Full coverage of baseball's unique and colorful terms will let you understand and speak the language as if you were born to it.

This homegrown sport is a part of every child's world, and our brand-new encyclopedia makes read-ing about it almost as fun as playing it!

Contents: Volume 4: Satchel Paige >> Switch-Hitter

■ *Paige was one of the Negro Leagues' best pitchers.*

Paige, Satchel

Leroy "Satchel" Paige pitched and pitched and pitched. After beginning as a teenager in the Negro Leagues in 1924, he was still throwing 41 years later in 1965. In between, he put together one of baseball's most amazing careers. However, except for only a few brief appearances in the 1940s and 1950s, that career did not include the Major Leagues, because of baseball's ban (until 1947) on African-American players.

Paige boasted an amazing fastball and an assortment of other odd pitches. He threw a curving "be" ball ("because it be where I want it to be"). He had a hesitation pitch, which he threw after pausing during his windup, frozen in place, before whipping the ball plateward. His arm seemed never to get tired. He pitched hundreds of games a year, first for several Negro League teams, then in exhibitions. He traveled thousands of miles to play ball, including playing in Mexico, Cuba, and the Dominican Republic. The records and statistics of all those games in all those places are not considered very accurate, so there's no way to know exactly how many games he won.

But win them he did. Though he couldn't play in regular games with the big leaguers, he played against them during the offseason. Hall-of-Famer Bob Feller called Paige the best pitcher he'd ever seen. Another Hall of Famer, Dizzy Dean, said he and Satch alone could have taken the Cardinals to the World Series. (Speaking of alone, one famous Paige story is that during exhibitions in a small town, he would call his entire team in from the field, then proceed to strike out the side, never letting the other team hit the ball.)

In 1948, when he was 42 (probably; no one was ever sure of his age), Paige finally made the Major Leagues. Owner Bill Veeck hired him for the Indians, and Paige went 6–1. He also won and saved games for the St. Louis Browns, and appeared in the All-Star Game for them. He had a quick stint with the Royals in 1965, making him, at the possible age of 59, baseball's oldest pitcher.

For his long career of success and personality, Paige was named to the Hall of Fame by a special committee in 1971. He died in 1982.

A FEW OF SATCHEL'S RULES FOR LIVING

Paige was famous for his sayings. Here are some of his best-known pieces of advice:

Avoid fried meats, which angry up the blood.

If your stomach disputes you, lie down and pacify it with cool thoughts.

Keep your juices flowing by jangling gently as you move.

Avoid running at all times.

Don't look back—something might be gaining on you!

Palmer, Jim

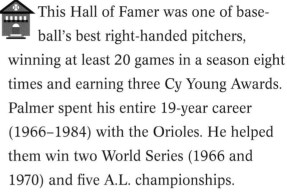 This Hall of Famer was one of baseball's best right-handed pitchers, winning at least 20 games in a season eight times and earning three Cy Young Awards. Palmer spent his entire 19-year career (1966–1984) with the Orioles. He helped them win two World Series (1966 and 1970) and five A.L. championships.

Palmer was well known for kicking his left leg very high and straight during his windup. He had a great fastball and a wicked curve. He was also an intense competitor and did his best in big games. In fact, he went his entire career without allowing a grand slam, showing how he could bear down in tough, bases-loaded situations.

Palmer was elected to the Hall of Fame in 1990 with one of the highest voting percentages (92.4) ever. A handsome man with a pleasing personality, he had a good career doing baseball commentary and TV commercials after his playing days were over.

Passed Ball

A pitch that gets past a catcher and allows a baserunner to advance. The official scorer at a game will decide whether or not a catcher should have caught or stopped the ball. If the scorer feels the catcher made the mistake, he'll call it a passed ball. If the scorer feels the pitcher threw the ball in a way that the catcher couldn't stop it, he'll call it a wild pitch.

■ *David Cone after his 1999 perfect game.*

Pennant

Slang for the championship of a league, division, or World Series. One of the early rewards for winning teams was a triangular flag, or pennant, that proclaimed the championship and was flown at the team's home ballpark. The name of this trophy, a form of which dates to medieval times, has come to mean the championship itself as much as the actual piece of cloth.

Pepper

A practice game in which several players toss a ball to a batter about 20 to 30 feet away. The batter then hits the ball softly back so that players can practice fielding. Because some of the hits by the batter might elude a fielder, you often see signs that say "No Pepper" at ballparks. This is for the safety of fans before the game, when a team might use pepper to warm up.

Perfect Game

A rare occurrence, this is when a starting pitcher does not allow a single baserunner to the opponent over the course of at least nine innings of a complete game. In more than 130 years of Major League Baseball, only 17 perfect games have been pitched. The first was by J. Lee Richmond in 1880 (the second just five days later!), while the most recent was by Randy Johnson in 2004. Only one perfect game has been thrown in the postseason. That came in Game Five of the 1956 World Series, when the Yankees' Don Larsen kept the Brooklyn Dodgers off the bases in a 2–0 win.

For a complete list of the 17 perfect games pitched through 2008, see the Appendix, page 86.

Perry, Gaylord

Hall-of-Fame pitcher Gaylord Perry is famous for two reasons, only one of which can be proven. The first is that he was a fine pitcher, the first one ever to win the Cy Young Award in each league (Cleveland in 1972 and San Diego in 1978). But he was also famous for supposedly throwing a spitball regularly. Such pitches have been illegal since 1920, but Perry was one of several pitchers who seemed to be able to get away with it.

A ball that is pitched with some sort of substance on it–saliva, tobacco juice, mud, Vaseline, etc.–can move in unusual ways. Pitchers who can control this pitch can succeed. In Perry's case, he was a great pitcher already. But when he started his "dance" on the mound, he made batters wonder if he was "doctoring" the ball, as the saying goes. He would tug his shirt or touch the front or back of his cap, or wipe his hand on his belt, then grab the ball. The uncertainty was enough for him to beat many batters.

He began his career with 10 seasons in San Francisco, followed by a solid stint with Cleveland. He later pitched for six more teams in a 22-year career that saw him win 314 games (and 20 games in a season five times). He was elected to the Hall of Fame in 1991.

Philadelphia Athletics

Please see Oakland Athletics.

Philadelphia Phillies

Please see pages 8–9.

Phillie Phanatic

The Phillie Phanatic is the large, fuzzy, green, strange-looking mascot of the Philadelphia Phillies. The Phanatic debuted in 1978 and quickly became one of sports' most famous mascots. Riding a small scooter, he whizzes around the field before games, doing tricks. During games, he visits with fans and helps them cheer.

■ *The Phillie Phanatic is one of baseball's most popular mascots.*

Philadelphia Phillies

Among all American pro sports teams, none have been playing for as long in the same place and with the same name as the Phillies. However, though they've been part of the National League since 1883, they've managed to win the world championship only twice, in 1980 and 2008. They have also won four other N.L. titles.

■ *Jimmy Rollins leads today's Phillies as their shortstop.*

The Phillies boasted some all-time heroes in their early years, but not enough to make them winners. Harry Wright, who had been part of the first pro team ever (the 1869 Cincinnati Red Stockings), managed the Phillies through 1893, but never finished higher than second. Not until 1915 did Philadelphia win the league title. However, they lost the World Series to Babe Ruth and the Red Sox. From then until 1948, the Phillies finished higher than sixth only once, often finishing last in the eight-team National League. They reached the Series again in 1950. That young team was known as the "Whiz Kids," and featured the pitching of Hall-of-Famer Robin Roberts. However, another World Series loss followed.

The Phillies boasted several top players in the 1950s and 1960s. Among them were slugging outfielder Richie Allen, speedy outfielder Richie Ashburn, and pitcher Jim Bunning. On Father's Day 1964, Bunning threw a perfect game against the Mets, the first one thrown in the N.L. since 1922.

Later in 1964, however, the Phillies had one of the most disappointing finishes ever. Leading the league by 6 1/2 games with just two weeks to play, they managed to blow it. They lost the entire lead and, with it, the pennant in one of baseball's biggest late-season collapses.

The arrival of a pair of Hall of Famers in the mid-1970s led to the Phillies' greatest run of success. Slugging third baseman Mike Schimdt combined home-run power with Gold Glove defense. He was a three-time MVP who would end his Hall-of-Fame career with 548 homers. Steve "Lefty" Carlton was a dominating pitcher who would win three of his four career Cy Young Awards while pitching for the Phillies.

Led by Carlton and Schmidt, Philadelphia won five division titles in eight years and two N.L. pennants. In 1980, the Phillies finally broke their championship drought. As all of Philadelphia cheered them on, the Phillies beat the Kansas City Royals in the World Series. Carlton had two of the team's four wins. Schmidt belted two homers and had seven RBI while batting .381. Nearly 100 years after the

■ *Chase Utley: a top second baseman.*

Philadelphia Phillies first took the field, they were finally champs. They returned to the World Series in 1983 and in 1993, but lost both times.

Another group of stars has helped the Phillies stay near the top of the National League in recent seasons, too. Slugging first baseman Ryan Howard was the 2006 N.L. MVP, while teammate Jimmy Rollins followed him in that role in 2007. Along with Chase Utley, a top-hitting second baseman, the trio helped the Phillies win the 2008 World Series over the Tampa Bay Rays.

PHILADELPHIA PHILLIES

LEAGUE: **NATIONAL**

DIVISION: **EAST**

YEAR FOUNDED: **1883**

CURRENT COLORS:
RED AND WHITE

STADIUM (CAPACITY):
CITIZENS BANK PARK (43,500)

ALL-TIME RECORD
(THROUGH 2008):
8,945–10,098

WORLD SERIES TITLES
(MOST RECENT): **2 (2008)**

Piazza, Mike

Most experts would agree that Mike Piazza, who retired early in the 2008 season, was the best-hitting catcher in baseball history. Oddly, Piazza almost didn't get a chance to play in the Majors. He was chosen in the 62nd round of the 1988 draft by the Dodgers only as a favor to Piazza's dad, a friend of Dodgers manager Tommy Lasorda. It turned out to be one of the biggest steals in draft history.

After several minor-league seasons, Piazza was the 1993 N.L. Rookie of the Year when he batted .318 with 35 homers. He finished second in the MVP voting twice in the coming few seasons and went on to bat above .300 six years in a row. His .362 average in 1997 was the highest ever by a catcher, as were his 201 hits. Other catchers had hit for average, while some had power, but no one had combined the two like Piazza.

After being traded to the Marlins in 1998 during a salary fight with the Dodgers, he was traded again to the Mets a week later. With the Mets, he kept up his hitting, helping them reach the 2000 World Series. He continued to make All-Star Games, but injuries and the hard work of catching slowed him down. After a year with the Padres, he wrapped up his career with a season as Oakland's designated hitter.

Piazza's career .308 average and 427 homers (including 396 as a catcher, the most ever) will make him a certain Hall of Famer when he becomes eligible.

■ *This baserunner is diving back toward first base to avoid being tagged on a pickoff play.*

Pickoff

When the pitcher or catcher throws to a base in an attempt to get a baserunner out–though not when the runner is trying to steal. Pitchers make pickoff attempts instead of throwing a pitch to the plate. These are most often thrown to first base. The main reason they are used is to help keep runners near the bag to prevent them from stealing. Pitchers who are adept at getting runners out this way or at least keeping them very close are said to have a good "pickoff move." Catchers make pickoff throws after receiving a pitch. They fire the ball to a fielder covering a base to try to catch the runners "leaning" the wrong way.

Pinch Hitter

A batter sent up to replace a player in the batting order. Pinch hitters can then take the place of the player in the field or be replaced themselves. The art of pinch hitting is a tricky one. Players might sit and watch a game for three hours and then be called off the bench to come through with a big hit at a crucial moment. Managers in the National League often use pinch hitters for their pitchers late in the game. Another reason for a pinch hitter is to have a right-handed batter face a lefty pitcher (or vice versa). The record for most pinch hits in a career is 212 by Lenny Harris. John Vander Wal of the Rockies had 28 pinch hits in 1995, the most ever for one season.

Pine-Tar Game

In 1983, George Brett hit a big two-out, two-run home run to put his Kansas City Royals ahead 5–4 in the top of the ninth inning of a game against the New York Yankees.

New York manager Billy Martin then asked the umpires to rule Brett out for having too much pine tar on his bat. This sticky stuff is legal for players to use to get a better grip on the bat, but they can't have it go too far up the handle. The umps ruled that Brett did indeed have too much pine tar on the bat and they called him out, removing the Royals' runs and giving the Yankees a 4–3 victory.

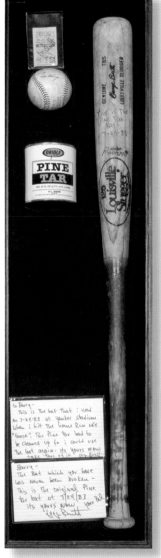

■ *Brett's famous bat on display.*

Brett's furious charge out of the dugout to argue, captured on TV, made the game famous. The Royals officially protested, and A.L. President Lee MacPhail agreed with them. He ordered the game replayed from that point, letting Brett's homer stand. The Royals ended up winning the wrapup, three weeks later.

■ *Pitchers start every play by throwing the ball.*

Pitcher

The player who stands on the pitching mound and throws the baseball toward the plate. The pitcher's job is to get the batters out, by striking them out or by getting them to hit the ball to the pitcher's teammates playing in the field. Pitchers throw with either their right hand ("righties") or left hand ("lefties" or "southpaws"). They choose from a variety of pitches to throw, from a straight fastball to a curveball that changes direction on its way to the plate.

The pitcher is often one of, if not the, most important player on a team when it's in the field. His success often plays a huge role in the success or failure of a team. If a pitcher can prevent the other team from hitting the ball in such a way that it scores runs, he gives his team a great chance to win. If, however, the pitcher struggles and walks many batters, allows many hits, and gives up several runs, then his team has to "dig itself out of a hole."

Pitchers today usually play one of three general roles. The starting pitcher begins the game. He will pitch five to nine innings every four or five days. Starters are the most dependable pitchers, with an ability to throw more than 100 pitches in each outing. Starters today rarely finish games they start. In the early days of baseball, starters finished almost every game. Some starters back then might pitch in 70 or more games; compare that to modern starters' totals of 25 to 35 starts per season.

Relief pitchers come in when starters get in trouble or get tired. Relievers only pitch a few innings at a time, and can thus pitch more often.

A closer is a special type of reliever who is brought on when his team is ahead, usually in the final inning. It's his job to "close" out the other team.

Pittsburgh Pirates

Please see pages 14–15.

Play Ball!

This classic phrase is used by the home-plate umpire to begin the game. When the home team on the field is ready and the pitcher is warmed up, the ump calls "Play ball!" to begin the action. He can also use this call to restart after any break in the game.

Playoff

A game or series of games held between teams trying to advance in postseason play. Up until 1969, when the first Championship Series games were held, the only playoffs in baseball were one- or three-game events used to determine a league champion after the regular season was tied. The first such game came in 1908, while other games were held in 1948 in the American League and 1951 and 1962 in the National League, for example. Today, Major League Baseball has four Division Series and two League Championship Series, all of which are called "playoff games."

Polo Grounds

The name of several homes of the New York Giants of the National League from 1883 to 1957.

Located in upper Manhattan in New York City, the most well-known Polo Grounds (1911–1964) was actually the third place with that name. Earlier Polo Grounds had been destroyed by fire. The Giants left for San Francisco after the 1957 season. The New York Mets played their first seasons in the Polo Grounds in 1962 and 1963.

Positions

The places on the diamond taken by a team playing defense are called positions. The traditional positions in baseball are first base, second base, third base, shortstop, left field, center field, right field, catcher, and pitcher. A player typically will specialize at one position, though some players can play several positions.

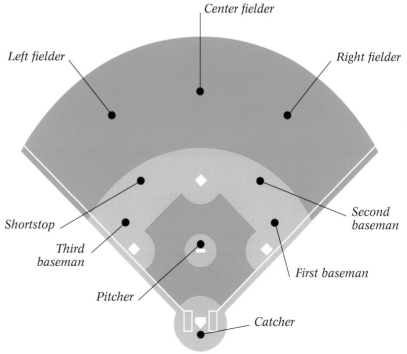

■ *These are the basic positions players take before each pitch.*

Pittsburgh Pirates

The Pittsburgh Pirates have been part of the National League since 1887, but have had only flashes of brilliance. Most of their seasons have been spent looking up at the leaders from down in the standings. They have boasted many all-time superstars, but few great moments.

■ *Honus Wagner: the greatest ever?*

The Pirates started off well, winning the league title in 1903 and playing in the first World Series (they lost to Boston of the American League). The Pirates won it all in 1909, led by one of the greatest players in baseball history, Honus Wagner. The big German-American player was a slugging shortstop, winning eight N.L. batting titles and leading the league in extra-base hits seven times. He also led the National League in stolen bases five times, and he played outstanding defense, too. Wagner could do it all, and he was one of the first five players named to the Baseball Hall of Fame.

The Pirates won it all again in 1925, led by a pair of Hall-of-Fame brothers, Lloyd and Paul Waner.

In the decades following that triumph, however, the Pirates were usually near the bottom of the N.L. standings. One highlight was the seven home-run titles won by out-fielder Ralph Kiner from 1946 to 1952.

In 1960, the Pirates created one of the most memorable plays in baseball history. It came at the end of the World Series, a Series that the Yankees dominated, but remained tied at three games each. In the first six games, the Yankees outscored the Pirates 46–17, but Pittsburgh hung tough, winning three close games. In the deciding game, the Pirates scored five runs in the eighth to take a 9–7 lead. But New York tied it 9–9 in the top of the ninth. Then in the bottom of the ninth, second baseman Bill Mazeroski hit the first (and still only) Game Seven, World Series-winning homer. The Pittsburgh fans and players went crazy, jumping and shouting. The homer by "Maz" regularly makes the lists of baseball's most famous hits.

Throughout the 1960s, the highlight for the team was the great play of Roberto Clemente. The rifle-armed slugger, who was born in Puerto Rico, was the first great player from Latin America. He faced some of the same prejudices that earlier pioneer Jackie Robinson faced and, like Robinson, overcame them. Clemente won batting titles four times in the 1960s, was the 1966 National League MVP, and won a record 12 Gold Gloves for his outfield play.

The 1970s were a great decade for the Pirates. In 1971, they won the N.L. pennant behind the batting skills of Clemente, the slugging and leadership of Willie Stargell at first base, and the pitching of Nelson Briles and Steve Blass. In the World Series for the first time in his career, Clemente shined. He was the Series MVP, batting .414. He did a postgame interview in Spanish, cementing his place in the hearts of Puerto Rican and Latino fans.

The Pirates won the N.L. East six times in the decade and capped it off with a return to the World Series in 1979. This time, Stargell, known as "Pops," was the clear leader. The team was a rocking, rousing group. The song "We Are Family" became the Pirates' theme, and the club won a hard-fought Fall Classic against Baltimore, with Stargell taking Series MVP honors.

■ *Jack Wilson is a top Pirates' player.*

With the exception of three division titles the team won when led by two-time MVP Barry Bonds in the early 1990s, not much good has happened on the field since with the Pirates.

Off the field, however, their fortunes have risen with the building of PNC Park, their new home. It opened in 2001 to rave reviews. Now the job of the Pirates is to bring the playoffs to their new field as well.

PITTSBURGH PIRATES

LEAGUE: **NATIONAL**

DIVISION: **CENTRAL**

YEAR FOUNDED: **1882**

CURRENT COLORS: **BLACK AND GOLD**

STADIUM (CAPACITY): **PNC PARK (38,496)**

ALL-TIME RECORD (THROUGH 2008): **9,691–9,480**

WORLD SERIES TITLES (MOST RECENT): **5 (1979)**

Power Hitter

A player who excels at hitting homers or extra-base hits earns this title. Power hitters are often large, strong players who are looked to by their team for big hits, including homers, in crucial situations.

Puckett, Kirby

One of baseball's most beloved players, Puckett had his Hall-of-Fame career cut short by eye trouble, and his life cut short by a heart ailment.

■ *Puckett celebrates his big Series homer.*

Puckett didn't look like a baseball player. He was shorter than most and rounder than most, but he also played harder than most. Puckett could flat-out hit, and he proved it by leading the American League in batting in 1989, the first right-handed hitter in 19 years to do so. In only 12 seasons, he had 2,304 hits.

Puckett also was a leader, helping inspire his team to World Series titles in 1987 and 1991. His most famous plays came during Game Six of the '91 Series. First, he robbed Atlanta's Ron Gant of a home run in the third inning, then he hit a game-winning homer himself in the 11th inning. Puckett's cheering, shouting run around the bases was a perfect example of his upbeat, positive personality. His baseball skills and his smiling attitude made him one of the most popular players of his day.

In September of 1995, Puckett was hit in the face by a pitch and missed the remainder of the season. In the offseason, he was diagnosed with glaucoma, an eye disease. His vision was so affected that he couldn't play baseball again. He was elected to the Hall of Fame in 2001, the third-youngest player ever inducted. Sadly, Puckett died of a stroke in 2006.

Pujols, Albert

Few players have ever started a career quite as successfully as Cardinals first baseman Albert Pujols [POO-holz]. In each of his first six seasons (2001–2006) he finished in the top four in voting for the N.L. MVP. He won the award in 2005. In his career, he has batted lower than .327 only once, and he has four seasons with 40 or more homers. He was the 2001 Rookie of the Year and has started the All-Star Game four times and been named to seven All-Star teams.

A powerful right-handed batter, he played outfield and third base before settling in at first base in 2004. (In fact, he has won Silver Slugger awards at three positions: OF, 3B, and 1B. The Silver Slugger goes to the top hitter at each of the nine field positions.) Pujols has improved his defense so much that he won the Gold Glove at first base in 2006.

■ *Pujols' powerful bat has led the Cardinals to five postseasons.*

In 2003, he won the Hank Aaron Award as baseball's top offensive player.

In 2004, Pujols had 46 homers and 123 RBI as he led the Cardinals into the World Series, where they lost to the Boston Red Sox in four games.

In 2006, however, Pujols topped even his own amazing marks. He had career highs in homers (49) and RBI (137) as he led St. Louis to another National League pennant. In the World Series against Detroit, Pujols finally added a ring to his growing collection of gleaming hardware.

In 2007 and 2008, he had his seventh and eighth straight seasons of 100 RBI with a .300 average or better and was among the MVP candidates again. Pujols remains one of baseball's most powerful offensive forces and is well on his way to becoming one of the greatest ever to play the game.

Radio, Baseball and

For baseball's first 60 years or so, the only way fans could experience a baseball game was by watching it in person. In the 1920s, however, that all changed with the invention of radio. Baseball's popularity helped make radio popular, too, as millions of people could listen in while baseball history was made every day and night.

The first Major League game on radio was broadcast on August 5, 1921, when the Philadelphia Phillies played the Pittsburgh Pirates. It went out on station KDKA in Pennsylvania. The World Series made its radio debut in 1922 on the same station and went nationwide the following year.

The game made for a perfect radio program. It was familiar to all the listeners, it had many natural breaks for commercials, and it was easily described by announcers. Some announcers, such as Grantland Rice and Graham McNamee, became household names across the nation.

By the 1930s, just about every team was broadcasting its games. Men such as Red Barber, Mel Allen, Vin Scully, and Bob Prince became the voices that carried generations of fans through the seasons.

When TV came along to stay in the 1950s, some predicted that radio would die out. However, it remains a vital part of many people's enjoyment of baseball. Many fans can't imagine a day at the beach in the summer without the ball game on the radio.

Today, many fans enjoy listening to their favorite teams' radio broadcasts via the Internet. Major League Baseball has a service that lets fans follow their favorites. They pay one fee and then listen to any game they want over their computers.

■ *Bob Uecker's voice brings the game to Brewers' fans.*

Rain Check

When a game is cancelled because of weather or some other problem, fans who had tickets to the game use this "rain check" to get a ticket to a future game at no cost, in return for the game they missed. You might hear the phrase used outside of baseball for anyone asking for a pass on a current event for a future one. For example, "I can't make it to dinner tonight, Carl. Can I get a rain check?"

Rally Cap

Baseball players are often superstitious. When their team is trailing late in the game and needs to score to tie or take the lead, players in the dugout might rearrange their caps to form different, and sometimes silly, shapes. This is supposed to bring good luck to their team. They might wear their hat inside-out, backward, or with the brim sticking straight up.

Ramirez, Manny

The hard-swinging slugger is one of the best right-handed hitters in baseball. He's also known for his quirky sense of humor and for the long, shaggy cornrows of hair draping out from beneath his baseball cap. But no matter what he looks like or how he talks, Ramirez can "rake," as the baseball experts say. In 2008, he became the 24th player in history to reach 500 homers for his career.

■ *Manny Ramirez shows off his power form.*

Ramirez began his career in 1993 with Cleveland. He was a big part of that team's return to the top of the American League. He helped the Indians win the A.L. pennant in 1995, whacking 31 homers, one of his nine seasons with 30 or more. He kept slugging, reaching 45 homers in 1998, while driving in 165 runs. It was the highest single-season total since 1938, as well as a Cleveland record. In his career, he has topped 100 RBI 11 times.

Ramirez signed a huge free-agent contract with Boston in 2000 and once again helped a team reach the top. In 2004, he smacked 45 homers and drove in 130 runs as the Red Sox won their first World Series since 1918. Manny was the Series MVP.

Though his total numbers were down in 2007, he helped them repeat the feat, as the Sox swept the Cardinals to win it all again. In 2008, Ramirez got No. 500. After feuding with Red Sox owners, Manny was traded to the Dodgers in July, 2008.

■ *Todd Jones was Detroit's "closer" in 2008.*

Throughout all the hitting have been the stories of odd behavior—what Sox fans called "Manny being Manny." He has gone inside the Green Monster in Fenway during time outs, he made baserunning errors, and he acted just a little goofy sometimes. But he still hits and hits, remaining one of baseball's most-feared sluggers.

Reese, Pee Wee

Harold "Pee Wee" Reese was a top shortstop in the 1940s and 1950s. He helped the Brooklyn Dodgers win seven National League championships in his 16 seasons in the league.

Reese got his nickname the game of marbles. (He was a champion player as a youngster, and a small marble is a "pee wee.") Reese joined the Dodgers in 1940, but missed the 1943–45 seasons due to military service in World War II.

Upon his return, his leadership, fine fielding, and speed on the bases all played a big part in the Dodgers' success. They won four more N.L. pennants in the years following the war, but lost in the World Series every time. The cry of "Wait 'til next year!" became famous, as the Dodgers' loyal fans awaited a title. Reese was one of the heroes of the team that finally won it all in 1955, defeating the Yankees in seven games. Reese retired in 1959 and became a coach and, later, a radio broadcaster. Pee Wee was elected to the Hall of Fame in 1984.

■ *The baserunning skills of Jose Reyes have made him one of baseball's most exciting players.*

Relief Pitcher

A pitcher brought in to replace the pitcher currently in the game. A manager might bring in a "reliever" because a pitcher is struggling or injured. In baseball's early years, relief pitchers were almost never used. The starting pitcher usually finished the game, no matter what happened or how badly he was doing. By the 1940s, more and more relievers were being used.

By the 1970s, "relief specialists" were on every team. Some might be used for longer stints, while others might only face a batter or two before being replaced themselves. In today's game, relievers include long relievers, situational relievers (i.e., left-handed pitchers brought in to face one lefty batter), setup men (usually used in the seventh or eighth innings), and closers.

Closers are the aces of the relief corps. They come on in the ninth, usually, to "close" the game with the score tight.

Reyes, Jose

Young Mets shortstop Jose Reyes has brought the stolen base back to baseball. In the years leading up to his debut in 2003, the home run dominated the game.

Jim Rice: a top 1970s slugger.

But Reyes and other young speedsters, such as Carl Crawford in the American League, re-introduced speed as an offensive weapon. Reyes was only 22 when he led the N.L. with 60 stolen bases in 2005. He was on top again in 2006 and 2007 as well.

Rice, Jim

In the 1970s, few hitters were more feared than Jim Rice. He was Boston's left fielder from 1974 to 1989. He took over that position from Hall-of-Famer Carl Yastrzemski and was an immediate star.

Rice finished second in the Rookie of the Year voting to Fred Lynn, his teammate on the Red Sox. By 1978, Rice was the league's MVP, with 46 homers and 139 RBI. Rice batted better than .300 seven times in his career, and he slugged 35 or more homers four times on his way to 382 in his career.

Rickey, Branch

Few people in baseball have made such a permanent mark on the world than Rickey. He was the general manager of the Brooklyn Dodgers who decided, in 1946, to bring an African-American player to the big leagues for the first time in the 20th century. On April 15, 1947, Rickey and Jackie Robinson made history when Robinson played first base for the Dodgers.

Breaking the "color barrier" was not Rickey's only contribution to baseball, however. The former catcher played a big part in creating the modern system of minor league teams being connected to Major League teams. He also made spring training a much bigger part of his teams' plans.

Rickey got his start in 1913 with the St. Louis Browns and moved to the Cardinals in 1919, for whom he was also the field manager. While with the Cardinals, he created the first "farm system" of minor leagues. He stayed with them until 1942, when he moved to the Dodgers, where he continued his innovations. The biggest was hiring Robinson, but he also made the

Dodgers' spring-training complex in Florida a model of organization and instruction. His players brought the fans of Brooklyn six pennants and the 1955 World Series title.

Rickey then ran the Pirates and brought on board many of the players who would win the 1960 World Series.

For creative leadership, for courage in the face of prejudice, and for turning baseball into a better business, Rickey often is considered baseball's best executive ever. He was named to the Hall of Fame in 1967.

Right Field

Looking from home plate, the area on the right side of the outfield.

Ripken, Cal Jr.

A Hall-of-Fame infielder with the Orioles for 21 years, Ripken will forever be known for one amazing feat: He played in a record 2,632 consecutive games. His record broke the mark of 2,130 set by Lou Gehrig. Ripken began his streak in 1982 and passed the record in 1995. He kept adding to it, finally sitting down and missing a game in 1998.

Ripken was one of the finest overall players of his era, winning two A.L. MVP awards and helping the Orioles win the 1983 World Series. Ripken also set a new standard for shortstops. He was one of the first players ever at the position who matched size—he was 6 feet 4 inches (1.7 m)—and offensive punch. Ripken belted 431 career homers. Plus, he set a record (since broken) by going 95 straight games without an error at one of baseball's toughest positions.

Ripken joined the Orioles in 1981 at the age of 20. His father, Cal Sr., was a longtime coach in Baltimore's minor leagues (he would later coach his son briefly as manager of the Orioles). By 1983, Ripken had slugged the Orioles to a World Series championship. He made the first of his 18 All-Star appearances that year.

■ *For nearly 16 seasons, nothing kept Ripken out of the lineup.*

Throughout his career, Ripken was praised by players, coaches, and fans alike for his positive approach. He was an easy choice for the Hall of Fame in 2007.

Ripken today helps organize a national youth baseball organization named for him. With his brother Billy, also a former Orioles' player, he also owns parts of some minor-league teams.

■ *Rivera has been dominant in postseason play.*

Rivera, Mariano

The dominant closer in postseason history, Rivera was a key part of the Yankees' great teams of the late 1990s and early 2000s. While he was excellent during the regular season—Rivera has posted six seasons with 40 or more saves, leading the league three times, and has earned eight All-Star selections—he has really nailed it in the postseason.

Rivera took over as the team's closer in 1996 and appeared in the postseason 12 seasons in a row. His career total of 34 saves in the playoffs includes a record nine in the World Series. He has also won eight games while losing only one. In addition, his postseason ERA of 0.77 is the best ever for a player with at least 100 innings. In New York's four-game sweep of Atlanta in the 1999 Series, he won one game and saved two others to earn the MVP award.

Rizzuto, Phil

Though not blessed with great size, Phil Rizzuto made up for it with great heart and tremendous hustle. In the 1940s and 1950s, "The Scooter" was the shortstop for one of baseball's greatest teams— the New York Yankees that won five World Series titles in a row (1949–1953). He was not an offensive star, but rather made his mark with outstanding defense. However, in 1950, he did hit .324 and won the A.L. MVP award.

Following his retirement in 1956, Rizzuto went on to a longer, and perhaps more successful, second career as a radio broadcaster. He was a part of Yankees' broadcasts from then until his retirement in 1995. His most famous phrase was "Holy cow!" Rizzuto was elected to the Hall of Fame in 1994.

Robinson, Brooks

Few players handled the "hot corner" better than Brooks Robinson, the third baseman for the Orioles for 23 seasons (1955–1977). That career ties for the most seasons ever with one team (with Carl Yastrzemski of Boston). Robinson made the All-Star team 15 times, and his 16 Gold Gloves are the most ever for a player other than a pitcher. Robinson's sterling defense helped the O's win four A.L. pennants and two World Series (1966 and 1970). He was also the 1964 A.L. MVP.

During several games of the 1970 World Series against the Reds, Robinson pulled off a series of amazing defensive plays that are still talked about today. First, he robbed Lee May of a hit by diving to stop a smash down the line. Then he turned a key double play on a drive by Tony Perez. And he later robbed Johnny Bench of a hit, too. It was a remarkable display, made even bigger by its timing in the World Series.

Robinson was named to the Hall of Fame in 1983.

■ *Frank Robinson as a young star for the Reds.*

Robinson, Frank

Slugging outfielder Frank Robinson was a star for two teams, belting 586 homers, still among the most ever. Robinson also made his mark on history by becoming the first African-American manager in the Majors when he took over the Cleveland Indians in 1975.

Robinson broke in with the Cincinnati Reds in 1956 when he was only 20 years old. He set a rookie record with 38 homers that year and just kept slugging, topping 30 homers in a season 10 more times. He helped the Reds win the N.L. pennant in

■ *Robinson signs his historic contract.*

Robinson, Jackie

Baseball players show courage when they face a great fastball or a collision with a catcher or an outfield wall. But Jackie Robinson showed courage of a very different kind by just stepping onto the field on April 15, 1947. Though he played that day with death threats hanging over his head, Robinson took that bold first step and changed baseball, sports, and America for good. As the first baseman for the Brooklyn Dodgers that day, Robinson became the first African-American player in the Majors in the 20th century. The "color line" was broken.

Robinson's path to that day was marked by success in everything he did. As a student at UCLA, he was the only person ever to gain a letter (play regularly) in four sports: baseball, football, basketball, and track and field.

Following graduation, he served in the U.S. Army. He then played for the Negro Leagues' Kansas City Monarchs. However, his skills, his intelligence, and his calm presence helped him catch the eye of the Dodgers' Branch Rickey. Rickey had it in mind to hire a black player for his team and break the scourge of racism in baseball. But he needed a player who would not fight back against the coming insults and anger. To fight back would give people an excuse to keep other black players out.

Robinson signed on and agreed to Rickey's terms. By 1947, after a season in Montreal in the minors, Robinson was ready. Amid national publicity and with many speaking against him—including some quickly silenced teammates—Robinson played with style, grace, and speed. He was the N.L. Rookie of the Year (the award was later renamed in his honor in 1997) and helped the Dodgers reach the World Series. Two years later, he was the league MVP, and he starred for the team for 10 years, batting .311 and averaging nearly 20 steals a year. After that first year, he played second base regularly. Throughout it all, he was a voice for his fellow black players and, later, for the emerging civil-rights movement.

Robinson was named to the Hall of Fame in 1962. He died in 1972. His number 42 was permanently retired by all Major League teams in 1997.

1961, and he played on eight N.L. All-Star teams for them. In one of baseball's most curious trades, in 1966, he was sent to the Orioles for pitcher Milt Pappas.

Robinson took his revenge on Cincinnati by winning the A.L. MVP award, becoming the only player to earn an MVP award in each league. He also completed the Triple Crown (leading the league in RBI, homers, and average), and helped the Orioles win the World Series. He played for the Dodgers and the Angels before joining the Indians in 1974. Robinson was appointed Cleveland's player-manager in 1975 for his historic first. Following his playing career in 1976, he was also the manager for the Giants, Orioles, and Expos/Nationals through 2006.

Robinson was elected to the Hall of Fame in 1982.

Rodriguez, Alex

Please see page 28.

Rodriguez, Ivan

A top defensive catcher, Ivan Rodriguez has won more Gold Gloves than any other player at his position: 13 through 2007. He has one of baseball's best throwing arms. Rodriguez also has a solid bat, with a career average above .300. He has earned 14 All-Star selections.

"I-Rod" started with the Rangers in 1991, when he was just 19. His best season was 1999, when he hit 35 homers with 113 RBI and was named the A.L. MVP. But he couldn't carry the Rangers beyond three wild-card berths. He moved to the Marlins in 2003 and helped them win a World Series. He joined the Tigers in 2004 and helped them win the A.L. pennant in 2005. Rodriguez is a certain Hall of Famer as one of the three or four best catchers ever.

■ *I-Rod's best weapon is his powerful throwing arm.*

Rodriguez, Alex

 Many experts consider Alex Rodriguez the best player in the game today (though some would argue for Albert Pujols). There is no argument, however, that "A-Rod" is one of baseball's best hitters. A three-time MVP, A-Rod has smashed numerous offensive records in his 15 seasons. For instance,

■ *Few players boast A-Rod's all-around skills.*

he has eight seasons with 40 or more homers, including three with 50 or more. In 1998, he became only the second player ever with 40 homers and 40 steals in one season. He had 10 straight seasons with 100 RBI or more, including five with 130 or more. He has five A.L. home-run titles and has led the league at least once in batting average, runs, slugging average, doubles, and total bases.

Want more numbers? In 2001, he signed the largest contract in sports history. The Texas Rangers agreed to pay him $250 million over 10 years. He was the MVP in 2003 while with Texas, even though the Rangers finished in fourth place. But he won the award thanks to 52 homers and 135 RBI.

But the Rangers were still not winning regularly, and they decided to move the slugger. He was traded to the Yankees for Alfonso Soriano and other players. The move paid off quickly for the Yankees, as he won the 2005 and 2007 A.L. MVP awards.

A-Rod played his first seven seasons with Seattle, debuting in 1994 as an 18-year former high school star from Florida.

Though he has dominated A.L. pitching for years, A-Rod is still looking for his first World Series ring. Seven times his teams have made the playoffs, but all lost there. Some say that A-Rod doesn't perform well "in the clutch." He's still out there slugging, however, and hopes to add a ring one day.

Rollins, Jimmy

 A versatile and talented short-stop, Jimmy Rollins was the leader of the Philadelphia Phillies' surprise drive to the 2007 N.L. East title. While batting .296 and stealing 41 bases, he was named the 2007 N.L. MVP. Not only a great player, but also a fiery leader, Rollins is a three-time All-Star. He kept it rolling in 2008, helping the Phillies win their first World Series since 1980.

Rookie

A player in his first full season in the Major Leagues. A player might appear in a few games during one season, but that might not count as his rookie season. He can become a rookie the following year by getting at least 130 at-bats or pitching 50 or more innings.

Rookie of the Year Award

The Baseball Writers Association of America gives the Jackie Robinson Rookie of the Year Award to the top first-year player in each league. Either a pitcher or non-pitcher can win the honor. The first ROY was Jackie Robinson in 1947. The award was named for Robinson, the Brooklyn Dodgers' great, beginning in 1997. It is an award a player can win only once. For a complete list of Rookie of the Year Award winners, see pages 84–85.

■ *Pitchers push off from this hard slab of rubber.*

Rose, Pete

Please see page 30.

Rounders

A bat-and-ball game played in England for centuries. Rounders was thought to be a sort of ancestor of baseball, but no direct link has been shown other than the general idea of a stick and a ball, which has been around for centuries.

Rubber

Literally made of hard rubber, this narrow horizontal slab is located in the center of the pitcher's mound. The pitcher's foot must be touching this slab when he begins a pitch. The rubber is anchored firmly in the dirt, so he uses it to push off and gain momentum toward the plate as he pitches. Fans might often see a pitcher using his cleat to dig a small hole in front of the rubber to gain more of this advantage of an anchor.

■ *Rose was nicknamed "Charlie Hustle."*

Rose, Pete

Rose is not only one of the most accomplished baseball players ever, he is also one of the most controversial. In 24 seasons with four teams, Rose got more base hits than any other player, ending his career with 4,256. He was the 1973 MVP and helped both the Cincinnati Reds and Philadelphia Phillies win World Series titles. He played in 17 All-Star Games, starting at four different positions. He later managed the Reds.

Unfortunately, Rose had a problem: He was a gambler. In 1989, Major League Baseball banned him from the game, saying that as Cincinnati's manager, he had placed bets on Reds' games. Gambling on the sport is against league rules and has been for decades. Because of the ban, Rose is ineligible for his well-earned place in the Hall of Fame.

In 2004, Rose finally admitted that he had indeed bet on Reds' games, but he said always for the Reds to win. However, even with that apology, he has not been taken back in by baseball, and his case remains controversial.

Rose was the 1963 Rookie of the Year with the Reds as a second baseman. From the start, he played with an all-out style that earned him the nickname "Charlie Hustle." He was a key part of Reds' teams that dominated the early 1970s and won World Series titles in 1975 and 1976. With the Reds, he won three batting titles and led the National League in hits six times. He reached 3,000 hits for his career in 1978 and 4,000 in 1984. In 1978, he had a 44-game hitting streak, the second longest in the 20th century.

Rose signed with the Phillies in 1978 and within two years had helped them win their first-ever World Series, though he was 39 years old by then. By 1985, he was back with the Reds. It was with them that he got his 4,192nd hit, breaking the all-time record set by Ty Cobb.

Rose was manager of the Reds from 1984 to 1989, when his gambling got him in trouble. He was one of the greatest players ever, but remains on the outside of the Hall of Fame, looking in with sadness.

Ruffing, Red

A move from the Red Sox to the Yankees in his sixth pro season turned Red Ruffing's career around. The Red Sox were terrible; the Yankees great. Ruffing flourished with great run support and was one of the top pitchers of the 1930s. He helped the Yanks win seven A.L. pennants and six World Series. Ruffing was solid in the post-season, going 7–2 in Series play. He won at least 15 games in 11 out of 12 seasons and posted two seasons with 20 wins. He was named to the Hall of Fame in 1967.

Run

When a player touches home plate after having gone around the bases—one at a time or all at once—he scores a run for his team. A "run" is how baseball players score for their team. A baseball game score of 5 to 2 means one team scored five runs and the other team scored two.

The career record for most runs scored is held by Rickey Henderson, who crossed the plate 2,295 times. Among players who played since 1900, the record is for most runs scored in a season is held by Babe Ruth, who scored 177 runs in 1921.

Run Batted In (RBI)

A player is credited with an RBI when a teammate scores as a direct result of the player hitting the ball. An RBI can be earned with a base hit, an out, a bases-loaded walk, or hit by pitch. The record for most RBI in a season is 190 by Hack Wilson of the 1930 Chicago Cubs. The single-game record is 12, reached most recently by Mark Whiten of the Cardinals in 1993. With 2,297 RBI, Hank Aaron is the career leader.

Rundown Play

When a baserunner is caught between two bases, the opposing team tries to tag him out. He can run and back and forth between the bases in an attempt to reach one safely. The process of throwing the ball

■ *An infielder chases a runner during a rundown play.*

Ruth, Babe

Any discussion of the greatest player in baseball history has to start—and often ends—with George Herman "Babe" Ruth. At first a dominating pitcher who helped the Red Sox win three World Series, he became the greatest slugger the game had ever seen. In the process, he made baseball into the National Pastime and made himself into one of sports' most legendary figures. His career total of 714 homers is third all-time to Barry Bonds and Hank Aaron. But as a measure of his greatness, consider that his 54 homers in 1920 were more than any other A.L. team of the time!

Ruth grew up in Baltimore, a rough-and-tumble kid with more energy than his parents could handle. They put him into a boys' school where he quickly excelled in sports, mostly baseball. He was signed by a local minor-league team, the Orioles, for whom he pitched and slugged. He joined the Major Leagues in 1914 with the Boston Red Sox and, by the next year, was a top left-handed pitcher. He won 18 games in 1915 and 23 in 1916 as the Red Sox won a pair of World Series titles.

In 1919, he split time between the mound and outfield—and set a single-season record with 29 homers. No one had ever seen a hitter like Ruth, who swung from the heels, aiming for homers. This was in a time

■ *Here's Ruth in 1920, his first year with the Yankees.*

that singles and bunts were more likely to be a part of a team's offense.

However, though he was clearly Boston's best player and destined for greatness, Ruth was sold to the Yankees in 1920 for cash. It was the worst move in Red Sox—and perhaps baseball—history. Ruth went on to lead the Yankees to seven A.L. pennants and four World Series titles. He did it by hitting more homers than anyone had ever seen. He had 54 in 1920 and 59 in 1921. That latter year, he also had 171 RBI while scoring 177 runs, the most by any player in one season in the modern era (post-1900). The man they called "The Sultan of Swat" was rewriting baseball history. After a few more seasons with big homer totals, he reached his peak in 1927, becoming the first man to hit 60 homers in a season. As part of New York's "Murderer's Row," Ruth led the Yankees to one of the most dominating seasons ever. They repeated as World Champs in 1928.

Ruth's numbers are amazing. He had 11 seasons with 40 or more homers, and 10 with 130 or more RBI. He led the American League in slugging average a record 13 times and homers 12 times. He topped .350 in a season eight times (though he won only one batting title in an era with many high-average hitters). More than all this, though, Ruth was an outsized personality. He smiled, joked, and kidded with men, women, and

■ *Ruth was honored at Yankee Stadium in 1948.*

kids. He said outrageous things, ate enormous amounts, and became baseball's first real superstar. Ruth's popularity carried baseball along to new heights.

He retired in 1935 after a short stint with the Boston Braves. He was one of five players named to the first class of the Hall of Fame in 1936. Though he never got his long-held wish of managing the Yankees, he remained a beloved figure until his death from throat cancer in 1948.

■ *Crash! On tag plays at home plate, the result is often a collision between catcher and runner.*

back and forth among fielders to try to tag the runner is called the rundown play. The play is sometimes called a "pickle."

Run Over the Catcher

Many of baseball's most exciting plays take place at home plate. When a baserunner arrives at home plate at the same time as the ball thrown in the from the field, the catcher must sometimes have to "block the plate." The runner can then run into or over the catcher in a thundering collision. It's a legal play, if a dangerous one. The catcher tries to hold on to the ball. The runner tries to knock it from the catcher's grasp.

Rusie, Amos

Few players can say that they changed baseball's rules, but Rusie can. A pitcher in the early 1890s, Rusie had a fastball so powerful that the pitcher's mound was moved farther away from the plate as a result. He recorded strikeout totals of 341, 337, and 288 from 1890 to 1892.

In 1893, baseball decided it had had enough of Rusie's powerful pitching. The rules makers decided to move the mound back from 50 feet (15.2 m) to its present distance of 60 feet, 6 inches (18.2 m). Rusie's mark of 341 strikeouts stood as the single-season record until Bob Feller had 348 in 1948.

Ruth, Babe

Please see pages 32–33.

Ryan, Nolan

Nolan Ryan blew away batters better than anyone in baseball history. A pitcher for an amazing 27 seasons for four teams, his record of 5,714 career strikeouts will probably never be matched. Nor may his total of seven no-hitters, three more than the player in second place. (As good as he was, Ryan could also be wild. He also holds the record for most walks, with 2,795–nearly 1,000 more than the pitcher in second place.)

Ryan started with the Mets in 1966 and was on the team that won the 1969 World Series. He moved to the California Angels and set a single-season record with 383 strikeouts in 1973. He would top 300 Ks (a nickname for strikeouts) in a season five times. Ryan won 15 or more games eight times, with a career high of 22 in 1974 with California.

With Houston from 1980 to 1988, Ryan kept up his power pitching. He helped the Astros reach the playoffs three times. He stayed in Texas to wrap up his career with five seasons with the Rangers, finally retiring at age 46 in 1993.

As for all those record no-hitters (he also had 12 one-hitters!), Ryan threw his first two in 1973. He had two more with the Angels, and one with Houston. After tossing one in 1990 at age 43, he topped himself with another in 1991 at age 44. He was the oldest pitcher ever to throw a no-hitter, and it cemented his reputation as a tough, powerful competitor.

Today, this Hall of Famer is president of the Texas Rangers and part-owner of minor-league teams.

■ *Ryan set a strikeout record with the Angels.*

■ *This player is "laying down" a sacrifice bunt.*

There are more than 6,700 SABR members worldwide. They include prominent writers and players, but also many fans—anyone who has an interest in baseball history. SABR's influence in recent years has been to make more people in the Major Leagues aware of more statistics (known as "sabermetrics") and their links to history and performance.

Sacrifice

A sacrifice is a bunted ball that results in the hitter being put out at first base (or reaching via an error or fielder's choice) while a runner or runners advance a base. The hitter, in effect, has "sacrificed" his turn at the plate for the good of the team. The hitter is not charged with an official at-bat on a sacrifice.

Sacrifice Fly

A sacrifice fly is similar to a sacrifice except that it is a fly ball that is caught, and an advancing runner must score on the play. This almost always happens with a man on third base, who tags up after the catch and races home. On rare occasions, a fast runner at second base can tag up on a very long fly ball and beat the throw home.

On a sacrifice fly, the hitter is not charged with an official at-bat, and he is

SABR

SABR is the abbreviation for the Society for American Baseball Research. It is pronounced like "saber."

SABR was founded in 1971 in Cooperstown, New York. Its mission is to "foster the study of baseball past and present, and to provide an outlet for educational, historical, and research information about the game."

credited with an RBI. A fly ball that results in a runner or runners advancing only to second or third base, but not home, is treated as any other fly-ball out. It is not a sacrifice fly, and the hitter is charged with an official at-bat.

Safe

When a player reaches a base without being called "out," he is "safe," that is, able to remain on that base. A runner is safe, for instance, if he touches a base before he is tagged by the ball. He is also safe if, on a force play, he reaches the base before the fielder with the ball touches the same base. Umpires decide whether a player is safe or out. If the call is safe, the umpire holds his arms out to the side, or waves his arms back and forth.

St. Louis Browns

This was the name under which the team that is now the Baltimore Orioles played from 1902 to 1953. The club was an original member of the American League in 1901 as the Milwaukee Brewers. The next season, the franchise moved to St. Louis. In 1954, the club relocated to its present home in Baltimore, taking the name of an older team. For a complete history of the franchise, see Baltimore Orioles.

Note: The Cardinals also were known for a time as the St. Louis Browns. The Cardinals' franchise originated as the St. Louis Brown Stockings in 1881 and joined the American Association in 1882. In 1883, the team became the Browns, and in 1892 joined the National League. The Browns became the Perfectos in 1899 before taking the name Cardinals in 1900. For a history of that franchise, please see page 38.

St. Louis Cardinals

Please see pages 38–39.

■ *The Browns and Cardinals meet with President Truman.*

St. Louis Cardinals

The St. Louis Cardinals are the most successful franchise in National League history, with 10 World Series titles. Among all big-league teams, only the A.L.'s New York Yankees have won more titles (26).

St. Louis' latest championship came in 2006. That year, the Cardinals rode the hitting of first baseman Albert Pujols (49 home runs, 137 RBI, and a .331 average) and the

■ *Stan "The Man" was a three-time MVP.*

pitching of right-hander Chris Carpenter (15 wins, a 3.09 ERA, and 184 strikeouts) to win the N.L. Central Division title. Manager Tony LaRussa's club won a modest 83 games during the regular season, but was the surprise team of the postseason. The Cardinals rolled past the San Diego Padres and the New York Mets to win the pennant. Then they needed only five games to beat the A.L.-champion Detroit Tigers in the World Series.

Pujols has become a superstar. He finished in the top 10 in the N.L. MVP balloting each of his first seven seasons entering 2008. That included 2005, when he won the MVP with a .330 average, 41 homers, and 117 RBI.

Pujols is just the latest in a long line of Cardinals' greats. That list includes Hall of Famers such as Rogers Hornsby, Frankie Frisch, Dizzy Dean, Enos Slaughter, Stan Musial, Lou Brock, Bob Gibson, and Ozzie Smith.

Hornsby was a player-manager for the 1926 Cardinals, which won the franchise's first World Series. The Cardinals had first fielded a team as the St. Louis Brown Stockings in 1881, and joined the American Association—a rival Major League to the National League—in 1882. The next year, the name was shortened to the St. Louis Browns. After the American Association folded in 1891, the Browns joined the National League the following season. In 1899, the Browns became the Cardinals.

The Cardinals struggled until Hornsby helped turn them around. A second baseman, "Rajah" was one of the greatest hitters in big-league history. His .424 average in 1924 is the best since 1900. He batted more than .400 three times and is the only player to win the N.L. Triple Crown twice.

After Hornsby, great players and championships went hand-in-hand in St. Louis. Future Hall-of-Fame second baseman Frankie Frisch was the N.L. MVP when the Cardinals won the 1931 World Series, and he was a player-manager for the team's '34 champs. The latter year, pitcher Dizzy Dean was the cornerstone of the team's "Gashouse Gang." His brother Daffy Dean also pitched for the Cardinals that season.

The Cardinals won three World Series in a five-year span from 1942 to 1946. Outfielder Enos Slaughter capped that stretch by making a famous dash from first to home on a single to win an exciting Game Seven from the Boston Red Sox in the '46 World Series. The real star of those teams, though— and the most beloved player in club history—was first baseman and outfielder Stan Musial. "Stan the Man"

played each of his 22 years in St. Louis. He won seven batting titles, was named the N.L. MVP three times, and made the All-Star Game every year from 1943–1963.

Speedy outfielder Lou Brock and fireballing pitcher Bob Gibson helped St. Louis win the World Series in 1964, then again three years later.

■ *Superstar Albert Pujols.*

In 1982, shortstop Ozzie Smith dazzled fans with his remarkable fielding and helped the speedy Cardinals win the World Series again.

Home runs came in bunches from slugger Mark McGwire. In 1998, he set a record with 70 homers.

McGwire's thrilling battle with the Cubs' Sammy Sosa that year for the home-run record electrified baseball fans. It has since lost some of its luster after both players came under a cloud of suspicion during the performance-enhancing drug scandal of the 2000s.

ST. LOUIS CARDINALS

LEAGUE: **NATIONAL**

DIVISION: **CENTRAL**

YEAR FOUNDED: **1881**

CURRENT COLORS: **CARDINAL RED AND NAVY BLUE**

STADIUM (CAPACITY): **BUSCH STADIUM (46,861)**

ALL-TIME RECORD (THROUGH 2008): **9,929–9,271**

WORLD SERIES TITLES (MOST RECENT): **10 (2006)**

■ *Gwynn was the best Padres' player ever.*

San Diego Padres

The San Diego Padres began as a National League expansion franchise in 1969. It took the Padres a long time to build a winning team. Once they did, though, they emerged as a force in the N.L. West in the late 1990s and early 2000s.

San Diego won four division titles in 11 seasons beginning in 1996, topped by a World Series appearance in 1998. They lost that Series to the Yankees, though.

That N.L. pennant was a far cry from the team's early days. Each of the Padres' first six teams (1969–1974) lost at least 95 games and finished in last place in the division. Those early teams had a couple of young stars in first baseman Nate Colbert and outfielder Ollie Brown. The team almost moved to Washington D.C. before the 1974 season. But Ray Kroc, the owner of McDonald's, bought the team and kept it in San Diego.

In Kroc's first season as owner, the team drew more than 1 million fans for the first time. San Diego featured Randy Jones, a young pitcher, and outfielder Dave Winfield.

Jones lost 22 games for the woeful Padres in 1974, but quickly developed into one of the best pitchers in baseball. He won 20 games in 1975 and 22 in '76, when he earned the N.L. Cy Young Award.

Winfield turned out to be even better. He earned four consecutive All-Star nods beginning with the 1977 season. His best year with the team was in 1979, when he hit .308 with 34 home runs and 118 RBI and finished third in the MVP balloting. In 1980, he signed with the New York Yankees as a free agent.

Winfield, shortstop Ozzie Smith, and relief pitcher Rollie Fingers—each of whom went on to the Hall of Fame—were the key players on the first winning team in Padres' history in 1978. The Padres didn't make the playoffs, though, until 1984. Manager Dick Williams' squad went 92–70 that year to win the N.L. West. Then the Padres beat the Chicago Cubs three games to two in a thrilling NLCS. The powerful Detroit Tigers beat San Diego in the World Series in five games.

After that, the Padres again lost more than they won until Bruce Bochy took over as manager in 1995. By Bochy's second season as manager, the Padres had won the West. They beat out the Dodgers by one game in a great race. Two years later, San Diego repeated as champs. After beating the Houston Astros and the Atlanta Braves in the N.L. playoffs, though, the Padres fell to the Yankees in four games in the 1998 World Series.

One man played for both of the Padres' pennant-winning teams. That was outfielder Tony Gwynn. He first came up in the summer of 1982, and he played his entire 20-year career in San Diego.

Gwynn, a soft-spoken star and a leader in the community, remains the most popular player in Padres' history. A remarkable hitter, he had a lifetime batting average of .338 and equaled Honus Wagner's N.L. record of eight batting titles.

Another popular Padres star is closer Trevor Hoffman.

■ *Brian Giles is a bright spot for San Diego.*

He was still with San Diego through the 2008 season. Hoffman saved an N.L.-record (since broken) 53 games for the Padres' 1998 pennant winners. He saved at least 30 games 13 times in 14 seasons beginning in 1995. In 2006, Hoffman became baseball's all-time saves leader.

By then, the Padres were playing their home games in the new Petco Park. San Diego won division championships in their new home in both 2005 and 2006. They fell to the Cardinals twice in the opening round of the playoffs. Bochy left to manage the Giants in 2007.

New manager Bud Black inherited a team featuring star pitcher Jake Peavy and 1B Adrian Gonzalez.

SAN DIEGO PADRES

LEAGUE: **NATIONAL**

DIVISION: **WEST**

YEAR FOUNDED: **1969**

CURRENT COLORS:
NAVY BLUE AND ORANGE

STADIUM (CAPACITY):
PETCO PARK (46,000)

ALL-TIME RECORD (THROUGH 2008):
2,933–3,421

WORLD SERIES TITLES
NONE

San Francisco Giants

In a long history that dates to 1883, the Giants have won 20 National League pennants and five World Series championships. Those totals are among the best in baseball history, although most of the club's success came in the first half of the 20th century, when the team was located in New York. The Giants have won several pennants since moving to San Francisco in 1958, but they are still looking for their first World Series title on the West Coast.

The Giants had some success in the National League's early years, winning a couple of pennants in the late 1880s. But it was after the arrival of manager John McGraw late in the 1902 season that they became the league's elite team. By 1904, "The Little Napoleon" had led the Giants to the pennant. He refused to play the champion Boston Americans of the young American League in the World Series, but the Giants played in their first World Series the next year. They beat the Philadelphia Athletics in five games.

Under McGraw, the Giants finished in first or second place in the National League 20 times from 1903 to 1931. They won the

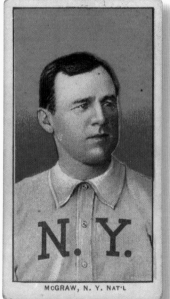

■ *McGraw made the Giants big winners.*

MCGRAW, N. Y. NAT'L

World Series three times: 1905, 1921, and 1922. Then, after Bill Terry took over as manager during the 1932 season, the club won the World Series again in '33.

Terry had been a hitting star on McGraw's teams. Slugger Mel Ott was another. Future Hall-of-Famers Christy Mathewson and Carl Hubbell were great Giants' pitchers.

But the biggest name in Giants history is Willie Mays. Fittingly, his career spanned the era of both New York and San Francisco. Mays was a rookie on the 1951 New York team that won the pennant, and was on deck when Bobby Thomson hit the "Shot Heard 'Round the World" to beat the Dodgers in a playoff that season. Three years later, Mays made perhaps the greatest defensive play in baseball history ("The Catch") when he snared a long drive by the Indians' Vic Wertz in Game One of the World Series. That sparked a four-game sweep that gave the Giants their last championship to date.

Mays could do it all on a baseball field. Any discussion of the greatest players in baseball history is sure to include him. Barry

Bonds' name is likely to come up, too. Bonds, who is Mays' godson, signed with the Giants in 1993. He already had won a pair of N.L. MVP awards with the Pittsburgh Pirates, then added five more in San Francisco to run his total to a big-league record seven. Bonds had a host of statistical feats, including most home runs in a season (73 in 2001) and in a career (762). But his records have been tarnished by suspicions raised in baseball's steroids scandal of the 2000s.

■ *Pitcher Matt Cain is a rising star.*

Bonds also failed to lead the Giants to a World Series title, although the 2002 squad came very close. San Francisco led Anaheim three games to two, but the Angels came from behind in Game Six, then took the finale.

It was another agonizing near-miss for San Francisco fans. In 1962, the Giants beat the Dodgers in a playoff for the N.L. pennant, but lost a seven-game World Series to the Yankees.

In 1989, the Giants won the pennant with an exciting, hard-nosed squad led by first baseman Will Clark. But the World Series against the Oakland A's is most remem-

bered for a devastating earthquake in the San Francisco Bay Area. After a 10-day delay, the A's completed an easy, four-game sweep.

These days, with Bonds no longer on the team, the Giants have turned to a youth movement featuring pitching and speed. Those traits are better suited to their waterfront ballpark, AT&T Park, which opened in 2000. Young pitchers such as Tim Lincecum and Matt Cain, and speedy outfielder Fred Lewis have Giants' fans excited about the future.

SAN FRANCISCO GIANTS

LEAGUE: **NATIONAL**

DIVISION: **WEST**

YEAR FOUNDED: **1883**

CURRENT COLORS:
ORANGE AND BLACK

STADIUM (CAPACITY):
AT&T PARK (41,503)

ALL-TIME RECORD
(THROUGH 2008):
10,256–8,814

WORLD SERIES TITLES
(MOST RECENT):
5 (1954)

Sandberg, Ryne

Ryne Sandberg, who made his big-league debut late in the 1981 season and played through 1997, was one of the greatest all-around second basemen ever

■ *Sandberg was one of baseball's top second basemen.*

and was a perennial favorite among loyal Chicago Cubs fans. In 2005, he was inducted into the Hall of Fame.

In 1982, the Cubs acquired Sandberg and shortstop Larry Bowa from the Philadelphia Phillies in exchange for shortstop Ivan DeJesus. It turned out to be an incredible steal for the Cubs. Bowa was nearing the end of his career, but Sandberg, who had had only six at-bats for the Phillies in 1981, soon turned into a star.

Sandberg took over the Cubs' second-base job in his first season in Chicago. The next year, he earned the first of nine consecutive Gold Glove awards for his defensive excellence.

After struggling at the plate his first two seasons, Sandberg blossomed into a hitting star as well in 1984. That year, he batted .314 with 19 home runs and 84 RBI. He led the National League with 19 triples and 114 runs scored, and helped the Cubs reached the postseason for the first time in 39 years. He was named the National League MVP. He was only the second second baseman since 1949 to earn that high honor.

"Ryno" also earned the first of 10 consecutive All-Star selections in 1984. He became an increasing power threat at the plate and drove in an even 100 runs in both 1990 and 1991.

His 40 homers in 1990 marked the first time since Rogers Hornsby in 1922 that a second baseman reached that mark.

Sandberg finished his career with a lifetime average of .285. He hit 282 home runs, including 277 as a second baseman. At the time of his retirement, that was the most ever by a player at his position.

San Diego Padres

Please see pages 40–41.

San Francisco Giants

Please see pages 42–43.

Santana, Johan

Johan Santana is often considered the best Major League pitcher of the 2000s. After playing eight seasons with the American League's Minnesota Twins, he was traded to the National League's New York Mets in 2008.

The native of Venezuela originally was signed by the Houston Astros when he was just 16 years old. He played in the Astros' and Marlins' organizations before making his big-league debut with the Twins in 2000. For several seasons, Santana bounced between a bullpen role and a starting role. In 2004, he broke out in his first full season exclusively as a starter. He won 20 games, led the league with 265 strikeouts and a 2.61 ERA, and earned the A.L.'s Cy Young Award.

■ *Santana was a big pickup for the Mets.*

After a 16–7 season in which he was third in the balloting, Santana won another Cy Young Award in 2006. His 245 strikeouts and 2.77 ERA led the league again, and he helped pitch Minnesota into the postseason for the fourth time in five years.

A left-hander who keeps hitters off balance with a strong changeup to complement his excellent fastball, Santana was a workhorse from 2004 to 2007. He pitched 912.1 innings in that span and struck out 983 batters while posting a record of 70–32. But the Twins, faced with the pros-

Francisco Rodriguez set a saves record in 2008.

Save

A save is a statistical category that credits the relief pitcher who finishes off a team's victory, usually in a close game.

By definition, only one save can be awarded in any game, and the starting pitcher in a game cannot be credited with a save. A relief pitcher earns a save if he is the finishing pitcher, but not the winning pitcher, in a victory by his team, and he meets any of the following situations:

➤ He pitches at least one full inning when his team has a lead of no more than three runs;

➤ He enters the game with the potential tying run on base, at the plate, or on deck;

➤ He pitches at least three innings.

Pitchers who specialize in getting saves are called "closers." In today's game, closers rarely are used for more than one inning.

The career record for saves is held by Trevor Hoffman, who had 554 through 2008. The single-season mark is 62, set by Francisco Rodriguez of the Angels in 2008.

pect of losing him to free agency following the 2008 season, sent him to the Mets in exchange for several young players. Santana quickly helped New York contend for an N.L. playoff spot.

Schilling, Curt

Right-handed pitcher Curt Schilling has won 216 regular-season games over a 21-year big-league career. But it is in the postseason that he has really forged his reputation, winning 19 games and helping his teams to four league pennants and three World Series championships.

The most memorable of those titles came with the Boston Red Sox in 2004. Boston hadn't won a World Series in 86 years, but Schilling–pitching with blood seeping through the sock of his injured right ankle–won Game Two of a four-game sweep over the St. Louis Cardinals. Three years later, Schilling won Game Two of another four-game sweep over the Colorado Rockies in the World Series.

A power pitcher, Schilling's 3,116 strikeouts through 2008 ranked 15th on baseball's all-time list. He fanned 300 or more batters three times, including a career-best 319 for the Philadelphia Phillies in 1997.

Schilling has pitched for five teams in his career, with his best seasons coming in Arizona in the early 2000s. He won 22 games and struck out 293 batters for the Diamondbacks in 2001 and won 23 games and struck out 316 batters in '02. His performances might have earned him the N.L. Cy Young Award either of those years,

■ *Schilling had postseason experience with the Phillies and Diamondbacks before he joined Boston.*

but Arizona teammate Randy Johnson was just as dominant and took home the trophy each time.

In 2001, Schilling and Johnson keyed the Diamondbacks' stunning, seven-game upset of the New York Yankees in the World Series. They shared the Series MVP award. Schilling won nine games for the Red Sox in 24 starts at age 40 in 2007

before an injured shoulder kept him out all of 2008. He was undecided about trying to make a comeback in '09.

Schmidt, Mike

Mike Schmidt was one of the greatest power-hitting third basemen of all time. He slugged 548 home runs for the Philadelphia Phillies from 1972 to 1989. In 1995, he was inducted into the Hall of Fame.

In just his second full season in the big leagues, Schmidt belted 36 home runs in 1974 to lead the National League. It was the first of 13 times over the next 14 seasons that he hit at least 30 home runs, and the first of eight times that he topped the league in homers. Only Babe Ruth, with 12 times, led his league more often.

In 1980, Schmidt had career bests of 48 home runs and 121 RBI to help the Phillies win the National League East. Then he batted .381 and had a pair of homers to help Philadelphia beat the Kansas City Royals in six games for the first—and still only—World Series championship in the club's long history.

■ *Schmidt used his powerful swing to crack 548 career dingers.*

That season, Schmidt also was the National League's MVP—an award he won again the following year, as well as in 1986. This 12-time All-Star was more than just a slugger, however. Schmidt was outstanding in the field, too: He won 10 Gold Gloves for fielding excellence. When he retired, he stood seventh on Major League Baseball's all-time home-run list.

Schoendienst, Red

Red Schoendienst was the scrappy, Hall-of-Fame second baseman for the St. Louis Cardinals' World Series champs in 1946. Two decades later, he managed the Cardinals to a World Series title.

Schoendienst was one of the best-fielding second basemen ever. In 19 seasons with the Cardinals, Giants, and Braves from 1945 to 1963, he led the National League in fielding percentage six times and earned 10 All-Star selections.

He could hit, too, batting better than .300 seven times—including .342 in 1953—and finishing with a career mark of .289. Plus, he led the National League with 26 stolen bases in his rookie season.

In 1965, only two years after finishing his playing career with just a handful of at-bats for St. Louis at age 40, Schoendienst took over as manager of the club. By 1967, he guided the Cardinals to the top of the N.L. standings. Then they beat the Boston Red Sox in a thrilling seven-game Fall Clas-

■ *Red's No. 2 was retired by St. Louis.*

sic. St. Louis returned to the World Series the next year, but lost in seven games to the Detroit Tigers. He managed in St. Louis through the 1976 season, then had brief interim stints at the helm at age 57 in 1980 and at 67 in 1990.

Schoendienst, whose given first name was Albert, wore a Major League uniform as a player, coach, or manager for more than 50 years. He was elected to the Hall of Fame in 1989.

SAN FRANCI

NO.	GIANTS	POS.	1	2	3	4	5
7	Benard 23 Burks - 3	8	4-3	◇	CS2-6	◇	◇
32	Mueller	5	9	◇	9	◇	◇
25	Bonds	7	HR	◇	3G	◇	◇
21	Kent	4	K	◇	◇	9	◇
6	Snow	3	◇	6-4	◇	PB 9	◇
1	Rios	9	◇	WP 6 FC	◇	7	◇
35	Aurilia	6	◇	9	◇	K	◇
29	Estalella	2	◇	SB BB	◇	◇	◇
48	Ortiz	1	◇	4L	◇	◇	◇
			◇	◇	◇	◇	◇

■ *Here's a section of a typical scorecard. Most fans have their own ways of keeping score, however.*

Scorecard

A piece of paper on which reporters and fans track the events of a baseball game. This includes the score, but it is much more than that. A set of symbols and numbers tells what each batter, pitcher, and fielder does over the course of a game. It is called "keeping score" or "scorekeeping." Before the extensive use of computers, these paper records were all that was used to record every event in a baseball game. They are the basis for many of the records

and statistics that are accepted as official today.

A scorecard also lists all of a team's players and coaches by name and uniform number so fans know who is in the game at all times and who is available to come off the bench and play.

Scouts

Scouts are employees of a baseball organization. Their job is to evaluate talent at all levels of play and report to the front office of a Major League team.

Scouts are trained to spot the characteristics of a baseball player—good and bad—that might not be noticed by the average fan. They watch players at the high school and college levels and can recommend whether a team should draft or sign them. Scouts also watch players in the minor leagues and on other big-league teams and offer analysis on possible trades or about players who will be playing against their team soon.

Scouts are also the "eyes and ears" of a baseball team as it seeks to learn more about future players and future opponents. They might watch a team play several games before that team faces the scout's team. Many scouts are former players, coaches, or managers.

Scully, Vin

No other broadcaster has been associated with one professional sports franchise as long as Vin Scully has with baseball's Dodgers. He worked his 59th season with the club in 2008.

Scully was 22 years old and the Dodgers were still based in Brooklyn when he began working alongside the famous Red Barber on the club's radio and television broadcasts in 1950. Barber left the Dodgers three years later, but Scully stayed on, even after the team moved to Los Angeles in 1958. He has been behind the microphone for many famous moments in Dodgers' history, including their lone world championship in Brooklyn in 1955, Sandy Koufax's perfect game in 1965, and Kirk Gibson's dramatic home run that won the opening game of the 1988 World Series.

For Gibson's homer, Scully was working for NBC Sports. It was one of 28 World Series that he has called on television or radio. Although Scully's tenure with the Dodgers has never been interrupted, he is also known to sports fans across the country for other roles. In addition to calling World Series games, he did Baseball Game of the Week telecasts, All-Star Games, and NFL football games on television and radio. He called the action when the San Francisco 49ers beat the Dallas Cowboys on "The Catch" in the 1981 NFC Championship Game.

In 1982, Scully was honored with the Hall of Fame's Ford C. Frick Award for broadcasters.

Seattle Mariners

Please see pages 52–53.

Seattle Pilots

The Seattle Pilots were an American League expansion franchise in 1969. After just one season, the team moved to Milwaukee and became the Brewers, who now play in the National League.

■ *Scully is baseball's most beloved play-by-play man.*

■ *Martinez was one of Seattle's best hitters.*

Seattle Mariners

The Seattle Mariners are the youngest team in the American League Western Division. They began play as an expansion franchise in 1977. In their relatively brief history, the Mariners have featured some of modern baseball's brightest stars, such as Ken Griffey Jr., Randy Johnson, Alex Rodriguez, and Ichiro Suzuki. None of those players, however, has been able to get the Mariners into the World Series.

The club's best season was in 2001. That year, Seattle won an incredible 116 games during the regular season. The Mariners lost only 46 times, and they breezed to the A.L. West title. After an opening-round victory over the Cleveland Indians, though, Seattle's title hopes were derailed by the New York Yankees in the American League Championship Series (ALCS).

Like most expansion teams, Seattle's history got off to a rocky start. The Mariners did not post a winning record in any of their first 14 seasons. There were some highlights, though. In 1979, the Kingdome, the Mariners' indoor ballpark, hosted baseball's All-Star Game. Three years later, veteran right-hander Gaylord Perry was pitching for the Mariners when he won the 300th game of his big-league career.

A turning point was 1987, when the Mariners selected Ken Griffey Jr., the son of the Atlanta Braves' Ken Griffey, with the first overall pick of the amateur draft. Then, in September, the team brought up third baseman Edgar Martinez from the minor leagues. Those two players soon would form the cornerstone of some winning teams in Seattle.

Two years later, Griffey was in the Mariners' Opening Day lineup. Martinez was still a third baseman, but eventually would be moved permanently to designated hitter, where he would become one of the best ever. And young left-handed pitcher Randy Johnson joined the club in a midseason trade with Montreal.

In 1991, manager Jim Lefebvre guided the Mariners to an 83–79 record. It was the club's first winning season. In 1994, 18-year-old shortstop Alex Rodriguez first played for Seattle. And in 1995, under manager Lou Piniella, another former big-league star, the Mariners had their most memorable season.

That year, the Mariners rallied from 11 games behind the California Angels in August. By October 1, the two teams were locked atop the standings. With Johnson on the mound for a playoff at the Kingdome, it was no contest. He struck out 12 and the Mariners pounded the Angels 9–1 to win the West.

After that, the Mariners stunned the Yankees in an exciting Division Series before the Cleveland Indians ended their title hopes.

Seattle won another division title in 1997 and earned a wild-card berth in 2000, the year they moved into new Safeco Field.

Then, in 2001, outfielder Ichiro Suzuki helped the club win another division title. Suzuki already had been a star in Japan. He became a star in America, too. In eight seasons through 2008, he never hit below .300 and he stole at least 30 bases each year.

■ *Ichiro has several hitting records.*

In the summer of 2007, Suzuki signed a contract extension to stay in Seattle through the 2012 season. Unfortunately, he has been the exception when it comes to keeping the Mariners' stars.

Seattle is a small-market city, and the franchise does not have the financial resources that other A.L. teams such as the New York Yankees or Boston Red Sox have. So the Mariners often have to trade talented players or let them sign for more money elsewhere as free agents. Still, it is a tribute to the organization that the club has continued to find good young players and often remains in the A.L. West title chase.

SEATTLE MARINERS

LEAGUE: **AMERICAN**

DIVISION: **WEST**

YEAR FOUNDED: **1977**

CURRENT COLORS:
NAVY BLUE, METALLIC SILVER, AND NORTHWEST GREEN

STADIUM (CAPACITY):
SAFECO FIELD (46,621)

ALL-TIME RECORD (THROUGH 2008):
2,376–2,683

WORLD SERIES TITLES
NONE

Seaver, Tom

Hall-of-Fame pitcher Tom Seaver was called "Tom Terrific." And for 20 big-league seasons, mostly for the New York Mets and the Cincinnati Reds, Tom was terrific. He won 311 career games, struck out 3,640 batters, and compiled a lifetime ERA of 2.86.

Seaver was a star in college at the University of Southern California before being drafted by the Atlanta Braves in 1966.

■ *Seaver was well-known for a delivery with a long stride.*

Commissioner Bowie Kuhn voided the pick, however, and the Mets were awarded Seaver's rights in a lottery. By the next season, the right-hander with the blazing fastball was a 16-game winner in the Majors and the National League's Rookie of the Year.

Two years later, Seaver was a 25-game winner. The Mets had never finished higher than ninth place before that season, but they won 100 games and shocked the A.L.-champion Baltimore Orioles to win the World Series. Seaver won the first of his three career Cy Young Awards, and was second in the N.L. MVP balloting.

In 10-plus seasons with the Mets, Seaver led the National League in wins twice, in ERA three times, and in strikeouts five times. In a game against San Diego in 1970, he set a Major-League record by fanning 10 batters in a row en route to a total of 19 strikeouts in the game, which tied another record at the time.

Midway through 1977, Seaver was traded for four players to the Cincinnati Reds, who were in a fight for the N.L. West title. He won 14

■ *The Yankees' second baseman "turns" a double play as an Indians' player slides into second—too late!*

of his 20 starts for the Reds, although they finished in second. In 1979, Seaver went 16–6, and Cincinnati won the division.

Seaver returned to the Mets for one year in 1983 before finishing his career with the Chicago White Sox and a short stint with the Boston Red Sox in 1986. At age 40 in 1985, he won 16 games for the White Sox, including a victory over Texas in late August to reach 300 wins for his career. Seaver was inducted to the Hall of Fame in his first year of eligibility in 1992. He received 425 votes of 430 ballots cast.

Second Base

This is the base on a direct line beyond the pitcher's mound and towards center field when looking at the diamond from the catcher's point of view. Just like its name says, it comes after first base in order.

Second base also can refer to a fielder on defense. The person who plays second base usually is positioned midway between the first-base bag and the second-base bag. The second baseman and the shortstop share the job of covering

■ *In 1973, the great Willie Mays ended his career with the Mets in Shea Stadium, which closed in 2008.*

the second-base bag. In scorekeeping, the second-base position is designated by the number 4.

Seventh-Inning Stretch

The seventh-inning stretch is a tradition at ballparks all over the country and at various levels of play. Spectators stand and stretch—and often sing "Take Me Out to the Ball Game"—after the visiting team has been retired in the top of the seventh inning and before the home team bats.

The origins of the seventh-inning stretch are not clear. The most popular version says that in 1910, President William Howard Taft threw out the first pitch in a game in Washington. After the top of the seventh, Taft stood to stretch his legs. Out of respect for the President, spectators at the game stood with him.

Baseball historians have uncovered references to a stretch-like tradition before 1910, however, so it is possible that the Taft version of the story has simply been exaggerated over time.

Shea Stadium

Shea Stadium served as the home of the New York Mets from 1964 through 2008. In 2009, the club was scheduled to move to the recently completed Citi Field.

After playing their first two seasons (1962–63) in the Polo Grounds, the Mets moved into their new home in the borough of Queens. It turned out to be a noisy location: Airplanes from nearby La Guardia Airport frequently crossed over the park on their flight paths.

Shea Stadium hosted the World Series four times, with the Mets winning in 1969 and 1986, and losing in 1973 and 2000. The latter loss came to the cross-town rival Yankees. Ironically, that team also played at Shea during the 1974 and 1975 seasons, when Yankee Stadium was being renovated.

Shortstop

Shortstop is one of the defensive positions. The shortstop is usually positioned on the infield halfway between second base and third base. The shortstop and the second baseman share the responsibility of covering the second-base bag. In scorekeeping, the shortstop position is designated by the number 6.

Shortstop is one of the most important positions on a defense.

For that reason, a good-fielding shortstop is more desirable than a good hitting shortstop—although several current Major Leaguers, such as Florida's Hanley Ramirez and the Mets' Jose Reyes, are good hitters as well as good fielders.

Shot Heard 'Round the World

In 1951, the New York Giants' Bobby Thomson hit a three-run home run to beat the Brooklyn Dodgers in a

■ *Derek Jeter is one of today's best shortstops.*

National League playoff and lift the Giants to the pennant. Thomson's blast was the "Shot Heard 'Round the World." It is also sometimes called the "Miracle at Coogan's Bluff." Coogan's Bluff overlooked the Polo Grounds, where the game was played.

The Giants had trailed the Dodgers by 13 1/2 games in the standings in mid-August before winning 37 of their last 44 games to force a three-game playoff. After the teams split the first two games, Brooklyn took a 4–1 lead into the bottom of the ninth inning of the deciding game.

■ *Thomson clubs his famous 1951 homer.*

New York's Alvin Dark led off the inning with a single against Dodgers ace Don Newcombe. Don Mueller followed with another single and, one out later, Whitey Lockman doubled in a run. With runners on second and third, Ralph Branca was brought in to pitch to Thomson. With the count one ball and one strike, Thomson delivered one of the most famous home runs in baseball history.

The radio call by Russ Hodges remains as famous as the hit: "The Giants win the pennant! The Giants win the pennant! The Giants win the pennant!"

Signs

Coaches and managers relay instructions to batters and baserunners through hand signals called signs. The catcher also uses signs to tell the pitcher what type of pitch to throw to the batter.

Signs can be simple or complicated. If there is not a runner on second base who could "steal" the signs, a catcher usually will put down one finger to instruct the pitcher to throw a fastball, two fingers for a curve, or three fingers for a changeup or other pitch. But if there is a runner at second base, the catcher will flash a series of signs. In that case, the pitcher must know what the real sign is, or what the combination of signs mean.

A third base coach might send a sign to a batter with a touch of the cap or a particular shout or even where he stands. Many times, he will go through a series of signs, most of which are intended to keep the defensive team from guessing what the real sign is.

Simmons, Al

As a rookie outfielder for the Philadelphia Athletics in 1924, Al Simmons hit .308 and drove in 102 runs. That was only the beginning. For each of the next 10 seasons, including two with the Chicago White Sox, Simmons again hit better than .300 and drove in more than 100 runs.

Despite an unusual batting style, Simmons was one of baseball's best hitters of the 1920s and 1930s. A right-handed hitter, he stepped toward the third-base dugout, or "in the bucket," when he swung; that earned him the nickname, "Bucketfoot Al." He batted a career-best .392 in 1926 and drove in a career-high 165 runs in 1930. That year, he also slugged 36 home runs while batting .381, and he led Philadelphia to its second consecutive World Series championship. Simmons was a staple in manager Connie Mack's outfield for nine years until being sold to the White Sox after the 1932 season.

After playing for several teams late in his career, Simmons ended his playing days back where he started, with the Athletics in

■ *A coach uses signs to let his players know the play.*

1944. He finished with a batting average of .334 and 1,827 career RBI. In 1952, he was inducted into the Hall of Fame.

Single

A single is a hit on which the batter stops at first base or advances beyond first base only with the aid of a defensive player's throw or error. Less commonly, it is called a "one-base hit." The word also can be used as a verb: "He singled to center field."

Not surprisingly, the man with the most career hits also has the most singles in big-league history—Pete Rose with 3,215 singles.

hit on the ground. It's hard for batters to hit a low, sinking pitch into the air as a fly ball.

Among current Major League pitchers, Arizona's Brandon Webb is probably the most successful sinker-baller. Webb won the N.L. Cy Young Award for 2006, was the runnerup in '07, and was one of 2008's top pitchers.

Sisler, George

"Gorgeous George" Sisler was a left-handed first baseman who played mostly for the St. Louis Browns from 1915 to 1930. He was one of the best players of his generation, and one of the best batters of all time. Sisler was described by *New York Evening Telegram* sportswriter Fred Lieb August 27, 1922 as "without doubt, the greatest player in the game today, greater than Hornsby, Ruth, and Cobb." Lieb wrote that at the end of a brilliant three-year run by Sisler. From 1920 to 1922, Sisler had 719 hits, and was the A.L.'s best-fielding first baseman. Sisler batted .420 in 1922. His 257 base hits in 1920 was a record that stood for 84 years, until Ichiro Suzuki of the Seattle Mariners broke the mark with 262 in 2004.

Sisler missed the 1923 season with vision problems and was never the same player after, although he played until 1930. He was elected to the Hall of Fame in 1939.

■ *Grady Sizemore shows off his powerful swing.*

Sinker

A sinker is a type of a pitch. It looks to the hitter like a fastball is coming from the pitcher, but the ball drops sharply as it reaches the plate.

Many pitchers throw a sinker. But a pitcher who specializes in throwing this pitch is known as a "sinkerballer." Sinker-ballers generally don't strike out as many batters as power pitchers, but they give up far fewer home runs because most balls are

Sizemore, Grady

Sizemore, who is a left-handed hitting center fielder, has been a mainstay of the up-and-coming Cleveland Indians teams of the mid-2000s. He was acquired in 2002 along with pitcher Cliff Lee as part of a six-player deal with the Montreal Expos for pitcher Bartolo Colon. Sizemore has proven to be one of baseball's best leadoff batters, with a rare combination of power and speed at the top of the lineup. He compiled an extraordinary 92 extra-base hits in 2006. Sizemore also has proven extremely durable, at one point playing in 382 consecutive games.

Sizemore made consecutive All-Star Game appearances in 2006, 2007, and 2008, and won a Gold Glove award for fielding excellence in 2007.

Slang

The language of baseball has developed over the past century from a variety of sources. Baseball slang is very colorful, and its roots come from all over. For example, a "Baltimore chop" is a batted ball that hits the ground near home plate and bounces so high that the batter very often beats the fielder's throw to first base.

Its origin comes from outfielder Wee Willie Keeler, who mastered the art in the 1890s with the original Baltimore Orioles.

A "can of corn" is an easy-to-catch fly ball. Storekeepers used to knock canned goods from a high shelf with a pole and easily catch it. A "Texas Leaguer" should be a "can of corn" but isn't, because it drops behind the infielders and in front of the outfielders.

If a batter gets good wood on the ball, he won't hit a "can of corn" or a "Texas Leaguer." He'll often hit a "line drive," which is a hard-hit ball that's not a grounder. A batter who fears an oncoming pitch and strides away from the plate as he swings is said to "step in the bucket."

■ *This outfielder is "hauling in" a "can of corn."*

Pitchers can prevent "line drives" by hitting the "paint." The "paint" is the outside edges of home plate. Good pitchers are said to "paint the corners."

Slang in baseball is constantly growing and evolving. The origin of the "Baltimore chop" may date back to 1890, but the usage of the "Mendoza Line" to describe batters whose averages stand above or below a .215 average dates only to the career of Mario Mendoza, who was a weak-hitting infielder in the 1970s.

Some slang seems outdated. Relief pitchers have been called "firemen" for decades, for their ability to come into games and "put out fires." But in recent years, managers use their relief aces to start innings, usually the ninth, meaning the closers can only put out fires that they create themselves.

For even more fun baseball slang, please see page 87.

Slide

The best way for a runner to avoid a tag and stop at a base without overrunning it is to drop to the ground and skid on one's buttocks. Most players tuck one leg under the other and reach out with their other foot toward the base. Some players also slide headfirst, diving to the ground and touching the base with their hands.

■ *This Phillies' runner is sliding in an attempt to reach the base before the Cubs player can tag him.*

A good place to practice sliding is in a sand pit or at the beach. That way, you can perfect the form without the pounding on your legs or on your clothes.

Slider

A pitch that is gripped more loosely than a curve so that the ball "slides" out of the pitcher's hand. It looks like a fastball but curves sharply just as it reaches the plate.

■ *Ozzie Smith was a "wizard" with a baseball glove.*

Slugging Average

This is calculated by dividing the total number of bases a player has reached on singles, doubles, triples, and home runs by his number of times at bat. It is used as a measure of a player's "power," or how often he gets extra-base hits. A player with a high slugging average is usually a powerful hitter. A good slugging average for a Major Leaguer might be .400 to .500. The all-time record for a single season was Barry Bonds, with an .863 mark in 2001. Babe Ruth holds the career record at .689.

Smith, Ozzie

The man known as "The Wizard of Oz" was a slick-fielding shortstop for the San Diego Padres and St. Louis Cardi-

nals from 1978 to 1996. He was an automatic choice for a Gold Glove, winning 13 in a row beginning in 1980. A 15-time All Star, Smith was one of the most popular players of his generation, sometimes doing back-flips as he ran onto the field.

Smith's first four seasons were played in San Diego, but after a trade with St. Louis, it was with the Cardinals that Smith won the only World Series championship of his career, in 1982.

Ozzie improved his offense enough to post nearly 2,500 career hits. His biggest hit came in the ninth inning of Game Five of the 1985 National League Championship Series. The switch-hitting Smith chose that moment to hit his first home run ever

one of the greatest defensive players in the history of the game. He was elected to the Hall of Fame on the first ballot in 2002.

Smoltz, John

John Smoltz is an almost-certain Hall of Famer, based on his two decades of pitching excellence for the Atlanta Braves. A native of Michigan, Smoltz was drafted by the hometown Detroit Tigers in 1985. But when the Tigers needed an established starting pitcher for the 1987 pennant drive, they traded Smoltz, then a 20-year old minor leaguer, for veteran Doyle Alexander. Alexander went 9–0 the rest of the season for Detroit and helped the Tigers reach the postseason, but Smoltz's heroics for the Braves would make the trade as one-sided as any in history.

Smoltz became one of three aces on an Atlanta pitching staff that led the Braves to 14 division titles and five World Series appearances. Smoltz was the National League Cy Young Award winner in 1996, when he won 24 games. He was always at his best in the postseason, compiling an impressive 15–4 career record. His postseason résumé is highlighted by Game Seven of the 1991 World Series. He threw shutout ball for seven innings, as did his mound opponent Jack Morris. Morris would eventually pitch a 10-inning, complete-game victory.

Smoltz missed the entire 2000 season due to injury, and when he returned he

■ *Smoltz has excelled as a starter and reliever.*

as a left-handed batter in more than 3,000 at-bats, ending the game and giving the Cardinals a 3–2 series lead over the Dodgers. Legendary St. Louis announcer Jack Buck called the game, and his famous call for Cardinals boosters to "Go crazy, fans, go crazy!" is remembered as one of the franchise's greatest moments.

Smith only hit 28 home runs in his 19-year career, but he did steal 580 bases. However, he'll be remembered for his work with the glove. He was unquestionably did so reinvented as a relief ace. Smoltz became the best closer in the National League, saving 154 games in little more than three seasons. In 2002, he broke the N.L. record with 55 saves. The Braves returned him to the starting rotation in 2005, allowing him to record his 200th victory and 3,000th strikeout.

Snider, Duke

Edwin "Duke" Snider will be forever known as "The Duke of Flatbush." He was one of the Brooklyn Dodgers' all-time greats, playing at Ebbets Field in the Flatbush section of town. Snider played with Brooklyn beginning in 1947 through its move to Los Angeles in 1958. Snider ended his career with the Mets and Giants.

Fans in New York in the 1950s debated about the three great center fielders for the Yankees, Giants, and Dodgers. Mickey Mantle, Willie Mays, and Duke Snider were the three men who shared a city and a position. Although Snider is generally considered to be on a level of talent beneath Mantle and Mays, Snider led the Majors in home runs and RBI during the 1950s.

Snider hit a career total of 407 home runs. Supplying the team's power from the left side of the plate, he led the Dodgers to six pennants in his first 11 seasons as a regular player. The Dodgers won the World Series only once, in 1955, with Snider slugging four home runs in the series.

Snodgrass' Muff

The Giants were three outs from winning the 1912 World Series against the Red Sox when center fielder Fred Snodgrass dropped an easy fly ball in the bottom of the 10th inning. That play has come to be known as "Snodgrass' Muff."

New York was protecting a 3–2 lead when Boston's Clyde Engle led off by lofting a lazy fly ball that Snodgrass missed.

■ *Duke Snider powered the Dodgers in Brooklyn.*

After a walk put the potential winning run on base, Tris Speaker lined a single to right field, driving in the tying run. Two batters later, the winning run scored on a sacrifice fly. Perhaps unfairly, Snodgrass received the blame for the Giants' loss. The name of his "mistake" remains famous among students of baseball history. Though he had an otherwise fine pro career, he lived with the mistake until his death in 1974.

■ *The U.S. softball team is among the world's best.*

Softball

A bat-and-ball game played like base-ball, but one in which pitchers throw underhand. Softballs are bigger than base-balls. The softball diamond has basepaths that are 60 feet (20 m) long, instead of baseball's 90 feet (30 m).

There are two basic games: slow-pitch and fast-pitch. Slow-pitch is played by all sorts of people. The ball is lobbed in a big arc toward home plate. Then a batter hits the ball and things move along pretty much like baseball. This game is played at many age levels by both men and women.

Fast-pitch softball is played at the international, pro, and college levels, most often by women. Pitchers whip the ball in underhanded, nearly as fast as some Major Leaguers. Hitters have to react quickly. Through 2008, soft-ball was part of the Olympic Games.

Soriano, Alfonso

Alfonso Soriano has combined power and speed as a leadoff batter for several teams since the early 2000s. He reached the double mile-stone of 200 career home runs and 200 career stolen bases in fewer games than any previous Major Leaguer.

Soriano joined the Yankees as an everyday second baseman in 2001 and hit a home run off Arizona's Curt

Schilling in Game Seven of the World Series, though the Yankees lost.

In 2002, he hit 39 homers and stole 41 bases, earning the first of six consecutive All-Star Game appearances. After another great season in 2003 with 38 homers and 35 stolen bases, he was traded to the Texas Rangers in exchange for Alex Rodriguez.

After two years in Texas, Soriano was traded to the Nationals. He had a career season in 2006, hitting 46 homers and stealing 41 bases, becoming the fourth player in history to join the select 40–40 club: 40 or more homers and steals in one year. (Jose Canseco, Alex Rodriguez, and Barry Bonds are the others.) In 2007, Soriano signed a long-term contract with the Chicago Cubs. In 2008, he helped them win the N.L. Central Division.

■ *Soriano has set new standards for combining speed and power.*

Sosa, Sammy

Sammy Sosa of the Dominican Republic hit 609 home runs–more than any foreign-born Major Leaguer–during a career from 1989 to 2007. He joined the Texas Rangers in 1989, and hit his first home run off of Roger Clemens. The Rangers traded Sosa to the White Sox in 1989.

Sosa was traded again, this time to the Cubs, in 1992. He became a beloved star in Chicago, becoming the first Cubs' player to ever hit 30 homers and steal 30 bases in the same season (1993). The Wrigley Field fans screamed in adoration when Sosa

■ *Giants pitcher Barry Zito is a left-hander—which makes him one of baseball's many southpaws.*

would sprint to his right-field position to start the game.

In 1998, Sosa captured the attention of the nation when he and Mark McGwire each surpassed Roger Maris' single-season home-run record of 61 that had stood since 1961. Sosa finished the season with 66 home runs, but it was McGwire who slugged 70 to set the new mark. Sosa won the Most Valuable Player award in 1998, and then came back to hit 63 homers in 1999. He hit 64 homers in 2001, becoming the only player ever to hit 60 or more in

three different seasons. Oddly, Sosa did not lead the league in any of his 60-plus home run seasons. Barry Bonds extended the record to 73 home runs in 2001.

After a brief stop in Baltimore, Sosa returned to Texas in 2007 and hit his 600th career home run, becoming only the fifth player in history to achieve the feat.

Southpaw

A word used to describe a left-handed pitcher. Why "south"? Because most ballparks are built so that home plate faces east so the afternoon sun does not blind a batter's eyes. Since the pitcher faces west, a left-handed pitcher throws the ball with his south hand, or his south paw.

"Spahn and Sain and Pray for Rain"

Gerald Hern, a sports writer for the *Boston Post*, wrote a poem to describe the importance of Warren Spahn and Johnny Sain to the 1948 Braves' pitching staff.

First we'll use Spahn,
then we'll use Sain,
Then an off day
followed by rain;
Back will come Spahn,
followed by Sain,
And followed,
we hope,
by two days of rain.

The poem was inspired by the dominant performances of Spahn and Sain during the Braves' 1948 pennant drive, when due to off days and rainy weather, the two pitchers combined to go 8–0 over a 12-day stretch.

Spahn, Warren

Warren Spahn won more games than any other left-handed pitcher in baseball history: 363 over a 21-year career spent mostly with the Boston and Milwaukee Braves from 1942 to 1965. Spahn won 20 or more games in a season 13 times,

including six straight years. He might have won more than 363 games, but he missed 1943 to 1945 due to military service in World War II.

Spahn lasted a long time in the Major Leagues, and he finished what he started. He led the National League in complete games seven straight years from 1957 to 1963. One reason was because he was rarely pinch-hit for. He belted 35 home runs, and he was one of the best hitting pitchers of all-time.

Spahn was the ace of the Braves' staff and helped lead the team to the World Series in 1948, 1957, and 1958. The Braves

■ *Spahn had a long and successful career.*

won the 1957 Series over the Yankees as Spahn won one game, and teammate Lew Burdette won the other three games.

Spahn pitched a no-hitter in 1960 at age 39, and pitched another no-hitter the next season. Besides being known as one of the best lefties ever, he will be remembered for his legendary windup and high leg kick. Spahn was elected to the Baseball Hall of Fame in 1973, his first year of eligibility, receiving nearly 83 percent of the vote.

Spalding, Albert

Albert Goodwill Spalding was one of baseball's best pitchers in the 1860s and 1870s. Later, he became even better known as the owner of a sporting goods company that stills bears his name.

■ *Pitcher-turned-businessman Albert Spalding.*

Spalding was the most successful pitcher of the first professional baseball league, the National Association, winning more than 200 games for the Boston Red Stockings from 1871 to 1875. Then he joined the Chicago White Stockings and started the A.G. Spalding Sporting Goods Company.

The National Association folded in 1876 to make room for the new National League. Spalding became the player-manager of the White Stockings. Among star players, Spalding was an early proponent of wearing a baseball glove, sparking a national trend. His store was equipped to manufacture baseball equipment, and success was rapid. Spalding was elected to the Hall of Fame in 1939.

Speaker, Tris

Tris Speaker, the "Grey Eagle," is one of baseball's greatest center fielders, remembered primarily for his defense. His work in the outfield must have truly been superior to overshadow his offense, for his .345 career batting average ranks as the fifth-best ever. Speaker played 22 years in the Major Leagues, and his 792 doubles still are the most all-time. He was also an outstanding baserunner, and stole 30 or more bases in seven seasons.

Speaker was known for playing a shallow center field, and for an uncanny ability to throw out baserunners. He had an amazing 449 career assists, among the highest totals of the 20th century. He began his career in Boston, where he, Duffy Lewis, and Harry Hooper formed the "Million-Dollar Outfield." They led the Red Sox to World Series championships in 1912 and 1915. Following the 1915 season, Speaker was traded to the Indians. He became the team's player-manager in 1919 and, one year later, he managed the Tribe to their first World Series championship.

In 1926, a gambling charge from 1919 against him and Detroit Tigers star Ty Cobb resulted in Speaker being forced to resign as Indians' manager. He was later cleared of all the charges. He finished his career as a player with the Senators and Athletics.

He was elected to the Hall of Fame in 1937, the second class ever enshrined.

■ *Speaker was one of the best of the early 1900s.*

Spitball

An illegal pitch thrown with saliva, sweat, or any slippery substance on the ball that makes it break more sharply. Spitballs were a legal pitch in baseball until 1920. Since then, a handful of players have been suspected or even caught putting stuff on the ball to make it move in odd ways. They have added Vaseline or pine tar, or they have used sandpaper or sharp edges to roughen up or cut the ball. All those things can make a pitch move in surprising ways.

If a pitcher is caught putting something on the ball, he can be thrown out of the game and later fined or suspended.

Split-fingered Fastball

A pitch thrown by holding the ball between the index and middle fingers with the fingers split apart as wide as possible. When thrown with a normal motion, the pitch will look like a fastball, but then break down as the batter swings over top of the ball. It's also known as a "splitter."

The pitch is a fairly recent invention. Former Giants pitching coach Roger Craig helped develop it. Several top pitchers of recent years, including Cy Young Award winners Roger Clemens and Curt Schilling, among others, have perfected it and made life tough for hitters.

■ *Here's Sportsman's Park during the 1946 World Series.*

Sportsman's Park

Sportsman's Park was a St. Louis ballpark that served as home to the National League's Cardinals from 1920 to 1966, and the American League's Browns through the 1953 season.

For most of its history, the ballpark favored left-handed power hitters who pulled the ball—thanks to a left-field fence that was closer to home plate than in most parks. Babe Ruth excelled here, hitting three home runs in Game Four of the 1926 World Series, and again hitting three home runs in Game Four of the 1928 Series.

Stan Musial played roughly half of his more than 3,000 games there, and no one but Carl Yastrzemski at Fenway Park played so many games at one ballpark.

In 1964, Sportsman's Park hosted the World Series for the last time. In Game Seven, Bob Gibson, the series MVP, pitched a complete-game victory as the Cardinals defeated the Yankees.

Spring Training

Major League teams get ready for each upcoming season by training and playing exhibition games during February and March. Teams that train in Florida play in the "Grapefruit League," while teams training in Arizona make up the "Cactus League."

Spring training dates back to 1870 when the Chicago White Stockings and Cincinnati Red Stockings set up camps in the South, where the weather in early spring is warm enough to play baseball.

Squeeze Play

When a batter attempts to score a runner from third base by bunting the ball. The play is called a "suicide squeeze" if the runner takes off before the ball is bunted, because if the batter misses the pitch, the runner will most likely be tagged out. That's called being a "dead duck." If the runner waits until the ball is safely bunted, it's called a "safety squeeze." A squeeze play can sometimes catch a defense by surprise and can be a quick way to add a run, especially if a team is not hitting the ball well that day.

Stargell, Willie

Willie "Pops" Stargell played for the Pittsburgh Pirates for 21 years, from 1962 to 1982. He led the Pirates to the World Series championship in 1971 against the Baltimore Orioles, and was the inspirational leader of the Pirates' club known as the "We Are Family" team in 1979, when the Pirates again met and defeated the Orioles in the World Series. In that 1979 season, Stargell shared the National League Most Valuable Player award with the Cardinals' Keith Hernandez.

Stargell led with his example as well as his bat. Though it was later in his career, the enthusiasm and energy he showed on and off the field, and the encouragement he gave his teammates, proved as big a part of the Pirates' win as his still-solid bat.

Stargell was an outfielder in the early part of his career, but moved to first base in 1972. He finished his career with 475 home

runs, which many believe would have been higher if he didn't spend the first half of his career playing home games at cavernous Forbes Field. He was elected to the Hall of Fame in 1988, the first year he was eligible.

Stearnes, Turkey

Norman "Turkey" Stearnes was a powerful left-handed hitting outfielder in the Negro Leagues in the 1920s and '30s. Also blessed with blazing speed, he got his nickname by the awkward way he ran the bases. Stearnes played for the Detroit Stars from 1923 to 1931, and then with the Chicago American Giants and Kansas City

■ *"Pops" Stargell was a Pirates' leader on and off the field.*

Monarchs before retiring in 1942. He had a .400 batting average in three seasons and led the Negro Leagues in home runs in seven different season. He was inducted into the Hall of Fame in 2000.

Stengel, Casey

One of the most colorful figures in the history of baseball, Charles Dillon "Casey" Stengel had a 14-year career as an outfielder with several teams from 1912 to 1925. His best years came in the early 1920s with the Giants.

Stengel, who acquired the nickname Casey because he was from Kansas City (or K.C.), was a good player who is remembered for entertaining fans during games. He once kept a sparrow hidden under his cap and at just the right moment tipped his hat to the crowd so the bird could fly away.

But it was as a manager that Stengel became a Hall-of-Fame figure.

After short stints with the Braves and Dodgers, Stengel was hired to lead the Yankees in 1949, and he won 10 pennants in 12 years. New York had an impressive collection of talent, including Mickey Mantle, Yogi Berra, and Whitey Ford. Stengel managed the talent, and then some. "The Old Perfessor," as he was also known, was a master of the art of platooning players at several positions.

continued on page 78

Steinbrenner, George

George M. Steinbrenner, a ship builder from Cleveland, led a group of investors that bought the New York Yankees from CBS in 1973 for a bargain-basement price of $10 million. The once-proud Yankees franchise was foundering, following nine straight losing seasons and falling attendance. Aided by the coming of free-agency, Steinbrenner would return the Yankees to prominence. Under Steinbrenner—whose reign is the longest ownership in team history—the Yankees have won 10 pennants and six World Series championships.

The man called simply "The Boss" is known for several things, most notably a hatred of losing and a short fuse. He hired and fired managers wildly, especially early in his ownership. The fiery manager Billy Martin was fired and re-hired by The Boss five times!

In 1974, Commissioner Bowie Kuhn suspended Steinbrenner from baseball ownership for two years after The Boss was indicted for making illegal contributions to President Richard Nixon's re-election campaign and then covering it up. The suspension was lifted after 15 months, with Steinbrenner returning to the Yankees in 1976. Under Steinbrenner's watchful eye, the

Yankees won three consecutive pennants beginning in 1976, and won the 1977 and 1978 World Series.

During these years, Steinbrenner did most of the work that earned him his hard-nosed reputation. He hired and fired manager Martin repeatedly, for example. He fired managers Bob Lemon and Yogi Berra only a few games into their seasons. He clashed with baseball reporters, too, who wrote often about Steinbrenner's methods of ownership.

■ *Steinbrenner (right) with former Yankees manager Joe Torre.*

In 1990, Steinbrenner was suspended again, this time for "life," by Commissioner Fay Vincent after the owner hired a gambler to dig up dirt on outfielder Dave Winfield when Winfield didn't perform in the clutch to Steinbrenner's liking. Steinbrenner was let back into baseball in 1993, and the Yankees have been a model franchise, and Steinbrenner a model owner, ever since.

The Yankees returned to the playoffs in 1995, the first of 13 consecutive postseason appearances. The "hire-and-fire" owner that Steinbrenner had been had mellowed, allowing Joe Torre to remain in the manager's office for 12 seasons, and leaving personnel decisions to his front office.

The new style worked, and Torre had a host of stars. He led the Yankees to World Series titles in 1996, 1998, 1999, and 2000. That gave the team 26 world championships, more than any other franchise.

Critics will argue with his methods, but the Yankees are now worth nearly $1 billion thanks to Steinbrenner's business skills. He was the first owner to sell broadcast rights of his team's games to cable television, an idea which has grown into the Yankees' own YES Network. Steinbrenner spearheaded a renovation of Yankee Stadium in the mid 1970s and is now overseeing the building of a new Yankee Stadium to open for the 2009 season, keeping the team in the Bronx.

In 2007, The Boss, aged 77 and in poor health, gave control of the team to his two sons, Hank and Hal.

Steroids, Baseball and

The drugs known as anabolic steroids were developed by scientists in the late 1930s to replace a chemical found in men called testosterone. Researchers discovered that laboratory animals injected with steroids experienced a significant increase in muscle growth. Bodybuilders and weightlifters began to abuse steroids, which led to abuse by athletes in other sports.

In the late 1960s, East German sports officials began giving powerful steroids to thousands of young athletes, resulting in the country winning a majority of swimming, gymnastics, and weightlifting gold medals at the 1976 Olympics. American athletes and trainers—along with the rest of the world—were quick to catch on: Steroids can increase an athlete's strength.

Initially, baseball players, who rely on flexibility, avoided anabolic steroids, thinking that the build-up of additional muscle mass worked against them. The prevailing wisdom changed in the late 1980s, according to Mark Fainaru-Wada and Lance Williams, writing in their book, *Game of Shadows*: "By his own account, the Typhoid Mary of steroid use in the big leagues was the Cuban slugger Jose Canseco, the first player to hit 40 home runs and steal 40 bases in the same season. Canseco

■ *Jose Canseco was the first player to reveal his own steroid use.*

said his own career proved that strength conditioning, when combined with steroids and human growth hormone [another chemical], translated into a higher batting average and more power. He claimed that the drugs could transform a good player into a great one."

The late 1990s and early 2000s saw a rash of records broken. More home runs were hit by more players and hit farther than ever before. Mark McGwire and Sammy Sosa, for example, both

■ *Rafael Palmeiro told Congress he didn't use steroids. He later tested positive and was suspended from baseball.*

cracked the 60-homer barrier in 1998, a mark only reached twice before. In 2001, Barry Bonds reached the current record of 73. As the records grew, however, many people suspected some players were becoming stronger through the use of drugs like steroids. However, it took a while before the league started to actually test the players.

The dangers of steroids were well known by the early 2000s. Baseball commissioner Bud Selig announced a program to study their health effects. By 2002, baseball banned steroids and other drugs. On December 13, 2007, former U.S. Senator George Mitchell produced the findings of his 20-month investigation into the use of steroids and other drugs in baseball. The report concluded that such drug use had been a big part of the Majors for more than a decade. The report put many new records into question. Fans began to believe that some players had cheated by using drugs.

By 2008, with newer, tougher testing in place, all signs pointed to steroids in baseball being on the decline. One piece of evidence: Since Bonds set his record, only six players have topped 50 homers and none have reached 60. However, the "Steroid Era," as the 1990s has become known, is still a time of great controversy.

Stengel had a funny way of expressing himself, and the media dubbed it "Stengelese." But it wasn't funny to him at all when the Yankees "retired" him following the 1960 World Series defeat, labeling him too old to manage. He was 70. "I'll never make the mistake of being 70 again," he said.

The expansion New York Mets hired him as their first manager in 1962, and he served as front man for a team of lovable

■ *Stengel guided the Yankees through 1960.*

losers he dubbed "the Metsies" for four woeful seasons.

Stengel's jersey No. 37 is retired by both the Yankees and Mets, and he was elected to the Hall of Fame in 1966.

Steroids, Baseball and

Please see pages 76–77.

Stickball

A form of baseball played on city streets. Stickball is played with a broomstick and a small rubber ball sometimes called a "spaldeen." The ball is pitched on one bounce and hitters get just one swing. Bases are usually cars or objects near the street. The game was very popular in New York City in the 1940s and 1950s, but is still played in some places today.

Stolen Base

A base gained by advancing when a batter does not hit a pitch. To steal a base, a runner first takes a lead off a base. Then, at the moment the pitcher starts his delivery to home plate, the runner sprints toward the next base. The catcher receives the ball from the pitcher and throws to a fellow fielder who is covering the base toward which the runner is headed. If the runner gets there first, he has stolen the base. But if he is tagged first, then he's out. Major League basestealers are successful about 70 percent of the time.

Rickey Henderson is baseball's all-time "thief," stealing a record 1,406 bases. He also set the single-season record in 1982 by stealing 130 bases.

Strike

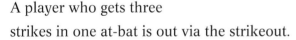 Any pitch that passes through the strike zone, or which a batter swings at and misses, or which a batter hits into foul territory (if he has fewer than two strikes on him). The home-plate umpire decides whether or not a pitch is a strike. A player who gets three strikes in one at-bat is out via the strikeout.

■ *Safe or out? This Indians' player is trying to steal second base.*

Strikeout

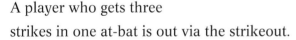 An out recorded when a pitcher delivers three strikes to a batter during one at-bat. A strike can be called by the umpire or recorded when a player swings and misses the pitch. A strike is also charged for the first two foul balls in a player's at-bat. A foul ball cannot be the third strike (unless it is bunted).

Among hitters, the career strikeout leader is Hall-of-Famer Reggie Jackson, with 2,597. The single-season mark is by Mark Reynolds, who "whiffed" 204 times during the 2008 season. For pitchers, No-lan Ryan holds both marks: 383 in 1973 and 5,714 for his career.

Strike Zone

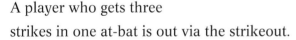 The area over the plate from the batter's knees up to his armpits. If a pitch passes through this area and also passes over home plate—and even if the batter doesn't swing at the pitch—the umpire calls a strike.

The strike zone is different for each player, of course, as each player is a different size. Umpires are not supposed to change the upper and lower points of the strike zone, even if a player crouches down to lower his shoulders.

What is and is not a strike is often the subject of fierce arguments during and after games among players and fans.

An interesting historical note is that in the early days of baseball (1860–1880), the batter could indicate whether he wanted a pitch to be above the waist or below. If a pitcher threw the ball over plate but not in the chosen zone, the pitch was a ball.

Submariner

A pitcher who throws with a motion that is lower even than sidearm. Very few pitchers can succeed using this motion. However, those that can—such as Kent Tekulve, Dan Quisenberry, and today, Chad Bradford—can be very difficult to hit. They seem to be pitching the ball from just above ground level.

■ *The white box shows this batter's strike zone.*

Sutter, Bruce

Bruce Sutter was a bearded, right-handed pitcher who threw a split-finger fastball, which made him one of the best relief pitchers ever. His prime came in the late 1970s, and early '80s. He saved 300 games, leading the National League five times, and at the time of his retirement in 1988, his saves total ranked third-best ever.

While pitching for the Chicago Cubs in 1979, Sutter saved 37 games, tying a then-N.L. record and winning the Cy Young Award, a rarity for a relief pitcher. Sutter was traded to the Cardinals following the 1980 season. He helped St. Louis win the 1982 World Series by saving two games in the Fall Classic. The single-season save record was pushed to 45 in 1983, which Sutter tied in 1984.

Sutter will be remembered in baseball history because he was among the first relief aces to be used almost exclusively in the ninth inning. He finished his career with the Atlanta Braves in 1988, and was elected to the Hall of Fame in 2006, in his 13th year of eligibility.

Sutton, Don

Don Sutton was a right-handed pitcher who won 324 games and struck out 3,574 batters from 1966 to 1988. He pitched for the Los Angeles Dodgers for 15 of those seasons.

■ *Don Sutton showing off his career-win total.*

As a 21-year old rookie in 1966, Sutton joined a formidable four-man rotation that included Sandy Koufax, Don Drysdale, and Claude Osteen.

It wasn't until the 1970s that Sutton became one of the best pitchers in the National League. From 1971 to 1978, only Tom Seaver had a better earned run average than Sutton, and only Seaver and Steve Carlton won more games.

Sutton was a big-game hurler. In 1974, in a best-of-five League Championship Series against the Pirates, Sutton pitched two complete-game victories for the Dodgers, allowing just one run in 18 innings. In 1982, he pitched the Milwaukee Brewers into the postseason by winning on the final

day of the season against the Baltimore Orioles' ace, Jim Palmer. In all, Sutton helped pitch his teams into the World Series four times: 1974, 1977, 1978, and 1982. He generally did well, but his teams were always on the losing end.

Sutton was suspected of scuffing baseballs and was frequently accused by opponents of throwing illegal pitches. Although he gained induction into the Hall of Fame, his Cooperstown credentials were a cause of debate because he never won a Cy Young Award and only once won 20 games in a season. But his consistency—he won at least 10 games in 22 of his 24 seasons— proved worthy to voters. This 324-game winner was inducted in 1998.

■ *Ichiro wears his first name on his jersey.*

Suzuki, Ichiro

Suzuki is a Japanese-born outfielder for the Seattle Mariners. He has been one of the best Major League players in the 2000s, after first spending nine years in Japan with the Orix Blue Wave. Ichiro, as he is known to his fans, became the first everyday position player from Japan to star in the Major Leagues.

Ichiro's father devoted his whole life to molding Ichiro into a model baseball player. Ichiro, though an excellent student, passed up college for baseball. He had a great career in Japan, where he won six league batting titles and was the Japan League MVP several times. His move to America was big news around the world of baseball. He was the best Japanese player yet to jump to America. At the time, many fans in both countries wondered if the former Japanese star would be overmatched in America. While some pitchers had made the jump, few hitters had.

The Japanese star quickly showed that he belonged in the American big leagues, despite not reaching the Majors until the age of 27. He made up for lost time, making the All-Star team each of his first eight seasons, and winning the Gold Glove seven times. He led the league in singles his first eight years in the Majors, and had more hits in his first eight years than any other player in big-league history.

In 2001, he was Rookie of the Year and A.L. Most Valuable Player. In 2007, he was MVP of the All-Star Game. Ichiro holds the Major League record for hits in a season, recording 262 in 2004 to break a record set by George Sisler in 1920. In 2008, by topping 200 hits for the eighth season, he tied an all-time record first set by Willie Keeler in 1901.

Ichiro is also an outstanding baserunner. He has stolen at least 30 bases in every one of his Major League seasons, and has topped 40 steals three times, with a high of 56 in 2001.

Sweet Spot

The place on the bat that has the best chance of delivering a hit. For most batters, this is an area a few inches long starting from the thick end of the bat and moving toward the handle. Pitches that are struck cleanly on this spot will usually travel the farthest. Pitches that hit off the end of the bat or off the thinner handle will have less power and go for less distance.

Swing Away

A phrase that tells a hitter to not worry about strategic hitting, but to just swing at the best pitch he sees. For instance, with a count of 3–0, many hitters will be told to "take," or not swing at a pitch, expecting that pitch to be ball four. In some situations, however, a manager will instruct the player to swing away–if the pitch is a good one.

Switch-hitter

A batter who is able to hit from either side of the plate. Usually, a switch-hitter will bat right-handed against a left-handed pitcher, and left-handed against a right-handed pitcher. A batter can switch between the two sides–though this is very uncommon–in the middle of an at-bat, but not after there are two strikes.

Switch-hitters are fairly rare, making up just over 10 percent of Major Leaguers. Perhaps the best switch-hitter ever was Mickey Mantle, whose 536 homers are tops in this group. Eddie Murray, another Hall of Famer, had 504 career homers. Among current players, the top switch-hitters include Chipper Jones and Lance Berkman.

■ *Atlanta switch-hitter Chipper Jones has a career .310 average.*

Rookies of the Year

The same year that Jackie Robinson shattered baseball's color barrier (1947), he also became the first player to officially be named top rookie in the big leagues (see page 29). That was the first season that the Baseball Writers Association of America (BBWAA) began voting for the Rookie of the Year. In 1947 and 1948, only one player was chosen as MLB's Rookie of the Year. Since 1949, a winner has been crowned from each league:

Year	Major League Baseball
1947	Jackie Robinson, 1B, Brooklyn (NL)
1948	Alvin Dark, SS, Boston Braves (NL)

Year	American League	National League
1949	Roy Siever, OF, St. Louis Browns	Don Newcombe, P, Brooklyn
1950	Walt Dropo, 1B, Boston Red Sox	Sam Jethroe, OF, Boston Braves
1951	Gil McDougald, 3B, N.Y. Yankees	Willie Mays, OF, N.Y. Giants
1952	Harry Byrd, P, Philadelphia Athletics	Joe Black, P, Brooklyn
1953	Harvey Kuenn, SS, Detroit	Jim Gilliam, 2B, Brooklyn
1954	Bob Grim, P, N.Y. Yankees	Wally Moon, OF, St. Louis
1955	Herb Score, P, Cleveland	Bill Virdon, OF, St. Louis
1956	Luis Aparicio, SS, Chicago White Sox	Frank Robinson, OF, Cincinnati
1957	Tony Kubek, SS, N.Y. Yankees	Jack Sanford, P, Philadelphia
1958	Albie Pearson, OF, Washington	Orlando Cepeda, 1B, San Francisco
1959	Bob Allison, OF, Washington	Willie McCovey, 1B, San Francisco
1960	Ron Hansen, SS, Baltimore	Frank Howard, OF, Los Angeles
1961	Don Schwall, P, Boston Red Sox	Billy Williams, OF, Chicago Cubs
1962	Tom Tresh, SS, N.Y. Yankees	Ken Hubbs, 2B, Chicago Cubs
1963	Gary Peters, P, Chicago White Sox	Pete Rose, 2B, Cincinnati
1964	Tony Oliva, OF, Minnesota	Dick Allen, 3B, Philadelphia
1965	Curt Blefary, OF, Baltimore	Jim Lebebvre, 2B, Los Angeles
1966	Tommie Agee, OF, Chicago White Sox	Tommy Helms, 2B, Cincinnati
1967	Rod Carew, 2B, Minnesota	Tom Seaver, P, N.Y. Mets
1968	Stan Bahnsen, P, N.Y. Yankees	Johnny Bench, C, Cincinnati
1969	Lou Piniella, OF, Kansas City	Ted Sizemore, 2B, Los Angeles
1970	Thurman Munson, C, N.Y. Yankees	Carl Morton, P, Montreal
1971	Chris Chambliss, 1B, Cleveland	Earl Williams, C, Atlanta
1972	Carlton Fisk, C, Boston	Jon Matlack, P, N.Y. Mets
1973	Al Bumbry, OF, Baltimore	Gary Matthews, OF, San Francisco

Year	American League	National League
1974	Mike Hargrove, 1B, Texas	Bake McBride, OF, St. Louis
1975	Fred Lynn, OF, Boston	John Montefusco, P, San Francisco
1976	Mark Fidrych, P, Detroit	Butch Metzger, P, San Diego
		Pat Zachry, P, Cincinnati (tie)
1977	Eddie Murray, DH, Baltimore	Andre Dawson, OF, Montreal
1978	Lou Whitaker, 2B, Detroit	Bob Horner, 3B, Atlanta
1979	John Castino, 3B, Minnesota	Rick Sutcliffe, P, Los Angeles
	Alfredo Griffin, SS, Toronto (tie)	
1980	Joe Charboneau, OF, Cleveland	Steve Howe, P, Los Angeles
1981	Dave Righetti, P, N.Y. Yankees	Fernando Valenzuela, P, Los Angeles
1982	Cal Ripken Jr., SS, Baltimore	Steve Sax, 2B, Los Angeles
1983	Ron Kittle, OF, Chicago White Sox	Darryl Strawberry, OF, N.Y. Mets
1984	Alvin Davis, 1B, Seattle	Dwight Gooden, P, N.Y. Mets
1985	Ozzie Guillen, SS, Chicago White Sox	Vince Coleman, OF, St. Louis
1986	Jose Canseco, OF, Oakland	Todd Worrell, P, St. Louis
1987	Mark McGwire, 1B, Oakland	Benito Santiago, C, San Diego
1988	Walt Weiss, SS, Oakland	Chris Sabo, 3B, Cincinnati
1989	Gregg Olson, P, Baltimore	Jerome Walton, OF, Chicago Cubs
1990	Sandy Alomar Jr., C, Cleveland	David Justice, OF, Atlanta
1991	Chuck Knoblauch, 2B, Minnesota	Jeff Bagwell, 1B, Houston
1992	Pat Listach, SS, Milwaukee	Eric Karros, 1B, Los Angeles
1993	Tim Salmon, OF, California	Mike Piazza, C, Los Angeles
1994	Bob Hamelin, DH, Kansas City	Raul Mondesi, OF, Los Angeles
1995	Marty Cordova, OF, Minnesota	Hideo Nomo, P, Los Angeles
1996	Derek Jeter, SS, N.Y. Yankees	Todd Hollandsworth, OF, Los Angeles
1997	Nomar Garciaparra, SS, Boston	Scott Rolen, 3B, Philadelphia
1998	Ben Grieve, OF, Oakland	Kerry Wood, P, Chicago Cubs
1999	Carlos Beltran, OF, Kansas City	Scott Williamson, P, Cincinnati
2000	Kazuhiro Sasaki, P, Seattle	Rafael Furcal, SS, Atlanta
2001	Ichiro Suzuki, OF, Seattle	Albert Pujols, 1B, St. Louis
2002	Eric Hinske, 3B, Toronto	Jason Jennings, P, Colorado
2003	Angel Berroa, SS, Kansas City	Dontrelle Willis, P, Florida
2004	Bobby Crosby, SS, Oakland	Jason Bay, OF, Pittsburgh
2005	Huston Street, P, Oakland	Ryan Howard, 1B, Philadelphia
2006	Justin Verlander, P, Detroit	Hanley Ramirez, SS, Florida
2007	Dustin Pedroia, 2B, Boston	Ryan Braun, 3B, Milwaukee
2008	Evan Longoria, Tampa Bay	Geovany Soto, Chicago

Perfect Games

Baseball's rarest pitching feat is the perfect game. A perfect game is when the starting pitcher completes the entire game without allowing a single baserunner. No hits, no errors, no walks, nothing–27 up and 27 down. The perfect game has happened only 17 times in baseball history through the 2008 season.

Date	Pitcher, Team	Opponent	Score
June 12, 1880	John Lee Richmond, Worcester	Providence	1-0
June 17, 1880	John M. Ward, Providence	Buffalo	5-0
May 5, 1904	Cy Young, Boston Red Sox	Philadelphia Athletics	3-0
Oct. 2, 1908	Addie Joss, Cleveland	Chicago White Sox	1-0
April 30, 1922	Charley Robertson, Chicago White Sox	Detroit	2-0
Oct. 8, 1956	Don Larsen, N.Y. Yankees	Brooklyn	2-0*
June 21, 1964	Jim Bunning, Philadelphia	N.Y. Mets	6-0
Sept. 9, 1965	Sandy Koufax, Los Angeles	Chicago Cubs	1-0
May 8, 1968	Catfish Hunter, Oakland	Minnesota	4-0
May 15, 1981	Len Barker, Cleveland	Toronto	3-0
Sept. 30, 1984	Mike Witt, California	Texas	1-0
Sept. 16, 1988	Tom Browning, Cincinnati	Los Angeles	1-0
July 28, 1991	Dennis Martinez, Montreal	Los Angeles	2-0
July 28, 1994	Kenny Rogers, Texas	California	4-0
May 17, 1998	David Wells, N.Y. Yankees	Minnesota	4-0
July 18, 1999	David Cone, N.Y. Yankees	Montreal	6-0
May 18, 2004	Randy Johnson, Arizona	Atlanta	2-0

Only perfect game in the World Series.

Baseball Slang

Baseball has been around for more than 150 years. In that time, the sport has gathered up a colorful assortment of words and phrases. Many are used away from baseball as well as within the game. Here are few interesting words and terms from baseball's dictionary.

ballpark figure   An estimate or general guess at a total. "I don't know how many coins I have, but I can give you a ballpark figure."

bees in your hands   A stinging sensation in the hands after hitting a pitch.

cheese   A fastball.

circus catch   A play by a fielder in which he catches the ball with a spectacular dive.

dead fish   A softly thrown pitch or a bunt that stops right on the grass near home plate.

ducks on the pond   Men on base for a batter to drive in, usually when the bases are loaded.

green light   When a coach signals a player to swing away. You often hear this term when the count is 3–0. Most players will be told to "take," or not swing at, the pitch. In some situations, certain hitters are given the "green light" to swing if they like the pitch.

hit a home run   In everyday use, it means to do something very well or to succeed to the highest level. "He really hit a home run with that report on spiders."

Hot Stove League   The offseason discussion of baseball. The term comes from the way in which old-time stores were heated. Locals would gather around the stove in the winter to chat about their favorite teams and players.

on the ball   A player who is doing very well, especially a hitter. In everyday use, this saying simply describes someone who is doing well or keeping their focus. "Joe was really on the ball today in math class; he knew all the answers."

pearl   A baseball fresh out of the box, still unused and perfect.

rhubarb   An argument between players and/or coaches and the umpires.

seeing-eye single   A ground ball that scoots just between infielders to reach the outfield.

the showers   The place where a pitcher is sent after he's taken out of the game; the clubhouse.

Uncle Charlie   A curveball (from its first letter "c").

Note: The authors thank author Paul Dickson for contributing The New Dickson Baseball Dictionary *to the world of baseball. It has given us—and might give you—hours of fun.*

*Read the index this way: "**4**:62" means Volume 4, page 62.*

Major League Baseball

Here's an easy way to find your favorite teams in the volumes of this encyclopedia. The numbers after each team's name below indicate the volume and page on which the information can be found. For instance, 1:14 means Volume 1, page 14.

American League

East Division		Central Division		West Division	
Baltimore Orioles	1:24	Chicago White Sox	1:62	Los Angeles Angels of Anaheim	3:26
Boston Red Sox	1:42	Cleveland Indians	1:68	Oakland Athletics	3:80
New York Yankees	3:68	Detroit Tigers	2:8	Seattle Mariners	4:52
Tampa Bay Rays	5:6	Kansas City Royals	3:14	Texas Rangers	5:10
Toronto Blue Jays	5:16	Minnesota Twins	3:50		

National League

East Division		Central Division		West Division	
Atlanta Braves	1:18	Chicago Cubs	1:60	Arizona Diamondbacks	1:14
Florida Marlins	2:36	Cincinnati Reds	1:64	Colorado Rockies	1:74
New York Mets	3:66	Houston Astros	2:72	Los Angeles Dodgers	3:28
Philadelphia Phillies	4:8	Milwaukee Brewers	3:48	San Diego Padres	4:40
Washington Nationals	5:30	Pittsburgh Pirates	4:14	San Francisco Giants	4:42
		St. Louis Cardinals	4:38		

About the Authors

James Buckley, Jr. is the author of more than 60 books for young readers on a wide variety of topics—but baseball is his favorite thing to write about. His books include *Eyewitness Baseball, The Visual Dictionary of Baseball, Obsessed with Baseball*, and biographies of top baseball players, including Lou Gehrig. Formerly with *Sports Illustrated* and NFL Publishing, James is the president of Shoreline Publishing Group, which produced these volumes. Favorite team: Boston Red Sox.

Ted Keith was a writer for *Sports Illustrated Kids* magazine and has written several sports biographies for young readers. Favorite team: New York Yankees.

David Fischer's work on sports has appeared in many national publications, including *The New York Times, Sports Illustrated*, and *Sports Illustrated Kids*. His books include *Sports of the Times* and *Greatest Sports Rivalries*. Favorite team: New York Yankees

Jim Gigliotti was a senior editor at NFL Publishing (but he really liked baseball better!). He has written several books for young readers on sports, and formerly worked for the Los Angeles Dodgers. Favorite team: San Francisco Giants.